UNLEASHING
the FORCE
of FAVOR

UNLEASHING
the FORCE
of FAVOR

Take Your Life to the Next Level

DUANE VANDER KLOK

Chosen
Grand Rapids, Michigan

Published by Chosen Books
a division of Baker Publishing Group
P.O. Box 6287, Grand Rapids, MI 49516-6287
www.chosenbooks.com

Printed in the United States of America

Library of Congress Cataloging-in-Publication Data
Vander Klok, Duane, 1953–
   Unleashing the force of favor : take your life to the next level /
Duane Vander Klok.
      p.   cm.
   ISBN 10: 0-8007-9398-6 (pbk.)
   ISBN 978-0-8007-9398-2 (pbk.)
   1. Kindness—Religious aspects—Christianity. 2. Service (Theology).
3. Helping behavior—Religious aspects—Christianity. I. Title.
   BV4647.K5V36 2006
   248.4—dc22   2006002886

Unless otherwise indicated, Scripture is taken from the New King James Version. Copyright © 1982 by Thomas Nelson, Inc. Used by permission. All rights reserved.

Scripture marked AMPLIFIED is taken from the Amplified® Bible, Copyright © 1954, 1958, 1962, 1964, 1965, 1987 by The Lockman Foundation. Used by permission.

Scripture marked GOODSPEED is from The Complete Bible: An American Translation, translated by Edgar J. Goodspeed and J. M. Powis Smith. Chicago: University of Chicago Press, 1939.

Scripture marked KJV is taken from the King James Version of the Bible.

Scripture marked MESSAGE is taken from The Message by Eugene H. Peterson, copyright © 1993, 1994, 1995, 2000, 2001, 2002. Used by permission of NavPress Publishing Group. All rights reserved.

Scripture marked NASB is taken from the New American Standard Bible®, Copyright © 1960, 1962, 1963, 1968, 1971, 1972, 1973, 1975, 1977, 1995 by The Lockman Foundation. Used by permission.

Scripture marked NEB is taken from The New English Bible. Copyright © 1961, 1970, 1989 by The Delegates of Oxford University Press and The Syndics of the Cambridge University Press. Reprinted by permission.

Scripture marked NIV is taken from the HOLY BIBLE, NEW INTERNATIONAL VERSION®. NIV®. Copyright © 1973, 1978, 1984 by International Bible Society. Used by permission of Zondervan. All rights reserved.

Scripture marked NLT is taken from the Holy Bible, New Living Translation, copyright © 1996. Used by permission of Tyndale House Publishers, Inc., Wheaton, Illinois 60189. All rights reserved.

Scripture marked ROTHERHAM is from The Emphasized Bible by Joseph Bryant Rotherham. Grand Rapids: Kregel Publications, 1959, 1967, 1971, 1974, 1976.

Scripture quotations marked YLT are from Young's Literal Translation, Robert Young, 1898. Public domain in the United States.

I dedicate this book to two amazing people who have been our friends for over thirty years: Bobby and Rose Bogard. Besides encouraging me to marry Jeanie those many years ago when I was having cold feet, they have supported and helped us in our journey from Bible school through ministry. Bobby was my executive pastor for thirteen years, helping me grow in favor as he contributed a healthy balance to my ministry with his gifts. He and Rose have been great examples of faithfulness, and my wife and I are very grateful for the favor they have shown us.

Contents

Acknowledgments

I would like to thank the staff and all the faithful volunteers who make our ministry not only possible, but also enjoyable.

I would also like to gratefully acknowledge writing consultant Trish Konieczny for her invaluable help in preparing this book for publication.

1

Turn On the Favor

Have you ever noticed how little the Bible mentions about the first thirty years of Jesus' life? God condensed what happened during those years into only two verses. If you had to condense thirty years of your life into two lines, what would be important enough to include?

In the two Scripture verses about Jesus' early life, God chose to emphasize the importance of favor: "Then he [Jesus] went down to Nazareth with them and was obedient to them. But his mother treasured all these things in her heart. And Jesus grew in wisdom and stature, *and in favor with God and men*" (Luke 2:51–52, NIV, italics added). To warrant a mention in these two verses, growing in favor must have been one of the most important developments in the Savior's young life.

Since Jesus is our example, growing in favor must be extremely important in our lives as well. When we discover what the "favor of God" is, understand that it is freely given to us and learn how to grow in it and realize its full effects, our lives will be changed dramatically.

Jesus knew how to unleash the force of favor. His life is the most powerful example we have of God's favor being fully released in someone's life.

Others in Scripture also operated within favor's mighty force.

Noah found favor with God and saved himself and his family from the flood.

Moses found favor with God and led God's people, the Israelites, as they followed God's presence to freedom.

Joseph found favor with both God and men. One day of favor in Pharaoh's court gained Joseph more than a lifetime of labor ever could have.

Ruth traveled with favor (her mother-in-law's name, *Naomi*, literally meant "the favor of God"), and she became the great-grandmother of King David.

Nehemiah found favor with the Persian king and rebuilt the walls of Jerusalem.

King David was so highly favored that he was called a man after God's own heart, and from his lineage came the Messiah.

What is this "favor" that was so important in their lives and that we so greatly need to experience in our own? One definition of the word *favor* is "the friendly disposition from which kindly acts proceed; to assist; to provide with special advantages; to receive preferential treatment." We all like it when kindness, assistance, special privileges and preferential treatment are directed our way! That is the favorable disposition God has toward each of us. The Creator of the universe Himself desires for us to enjoy this kind of relationship with Him. He loves us: "If God didn't hesitate to put everything on the line for us, embracing our condition and exposing himself to the worst by sending his own Son, is there anything else he wouldn't gladly and freely do for us?" (Romans 8:32, MESSAGE).

God *wants* to bless us, assist us and give us preferential treatment and special advantages in life. Not only that, but when we are fully enjoying God's favor, He also increases our favor with other people: "When a man's ways please the LORD, He makes even his enemies to be at peace with him" (Proverbs 16:7).

Favor makes a tremendous difference in life. When we begin to walk in higher degrees or levels of favor, we experience a flood of blessings. God protects us, opens doors for us that otherwise would be shut, pours out financial increase, gives us health and healing, helps us find new ways to bless others and kindly disposes other people toward us. As a result, people are stirred to give us preferential treatment, promote us and help us succeed.

Every area of our lives will be changed as we allow favor to be released in our lives. And it is possible for us to grow in this favor with both God and men, as Jesus did. We first need to realize, though, that favor is not automatic. We need to take action to see its full force unleashed. Any believer can learn how to take the steps necessary to grow in favor—it is simply a matter of knowing how favor works.

How the Force of Favor Works

The force of God's favor works the same way as electricity. The electrical system wired throughout a home surrounds the owner all the time, but the owner must flip a switch to release its power. God's favor surrounds us all the time, too: "For surely, O LORD, you bless the righteous; you surround them with your favor as with a shield" (Psalm 5:12, NIV). But even though we are surrounded by favor, some of us are not yet walking in all the favor God has for us because we have neglected to make the connection or hit the switch to release it. When we actively apply what the Bible teaches us about God's favor, we hit the "favor switch" and enable the full force of God's favor to powerfully affect our lives.

Now, I could walk into my home every day of the week and never turn on a light. All that electrical force would still surround me, but I would not benefit from its power. My lights are not automatic. Even when they are working perfectly, I still have to hit a switch to turn them on. Neither is the full force of God's favor automatic.

And just as there are different voltage levels of electrical force, there are different levels of favor. You can live your whole Christian life surrounded by supernatural favor but never hit the switch to experience the full force of its power. You may experience the beginning of favor—knowing you are saved by God's grace. That is amazing in itself, but it is not by any means all the favor God has in store for you. When the full force of God's favor is unleashed in your life, you will recognize what a difference it makes. But it does not strike by chance. There are choices you make that position you to fully benefit from favor's awesome power. You can align yourself with the flow of favor by discovering what God says about it in His Word.

You can take specific steps to walk in agreement with God's Word about favor and exercise your faith for it. First, *expect* God's favor simply because He loves His children. Then *believe* that He means to bless you personally with favor. Next, *confess* by faith that He is releasing favor into your life. We will map out these steps in more detail in the chapters ahead.

Favor Is Free for the Asking

For years now, I have not left my house a single day without first praying for favor. Prayer is the best place to start when you want to grow in favor. I ask God for an abundance of His favor every day. God has an abundance to give, and each morning is a great time to ask for it.

According to Ruth 2:16, Ruth found favor with Boaz, and he directed his men to let handfuls of grain fall on purpose for her to glean. I confess "handfuls on purpose" for my family. I thank God for surrounding us with favor as with a shield (see Psalm 5:12) and for crowning each of us with glory and favor ("glory and honor" in Psalm 8:5 can also be translated "glory and favor"). I pray for each family member by name: "Lord, surround Jeanie with favor as with a shield. Lord, crown Stephanie with glory and favor. . . ."

Later in the day, I might find myself on a tight schedule. Needing to make a quick—at least I hope quick—stop at the store, I start feeling rushed. As I think about how much longer I will be standing in the checkout line, a cashier approaches and says, "I'm just opening up my aisle. Please step over; I can help you." I step to the front, knowing God's favor is at work.

Favor is free for the asking, as Jesus announced one Sabbath day when He read aloud in the synagogue of Nazareth, His hometown:

> And there was handed to Him [the roll of] the book of the prophet Isaiah. He opened (unrolled) the book and found the place where it was written,
>
> The Spirit of the Lord [is] upon Me, because He has anointed Me [the Anointed One, the Messiah] to preach the good news (the Gospel) to the poor; He has sent Me to announce release to the captives and recovery of sight to the blind, to send forth as delivered those who

are oppressed [who are downtrodden, bruised, crushed, and broken down by calamity],

To proclaim the accepted and acceptable year of the Lord [the day when salvation *and the free favors of God profusely abound*].

Luke 4:17–19, AMPLIFIED (italics added)

One of the purposes of Jesus' ministry, then, was to proclaim that in the time of salvation the free favors of God would profusely abound. If you know His salvation, then those favors are yours today. (And if you have not experienced salvation, you can do so now. If you do not know for sure that if your heart stopped beating you would be on your way to heaven, see the appendix on page 139 for help on how you *can* know that for sure.)

Praying for favor and then bypassing a long checkout line may not be an earthshaking event, but add several such incidents together in a day and you know you are walking in supernatural favor. Sometimes, though, the incidents are not so small! During the time when I was preaching a series of messages on the force of favor, a couple approached me after a service. They wanted to tell me their true story about how God had answered a prayer for favor.

"I don't normally come to church," the husband confessed to me, "but yesterday before I left the house to go to my niece's and cut down some trees, my wife prayed for me. She prayed that favor would be around me like a shield. Then I climbed into my pickup truck and drove away, pulling a trailer with my tractor and all my tools in it. It was a foggy morning, and somehow I missed seeing the train. I hit the brakes and tried to swerve, but a thin coating of ice on the road and the heavy tractor on the trailer pushed me right into the train! I hit that train at sixty miles an hour," he said as he shook his head in amazement. "It dragged my truck right down the tracks with it until the trailer caught on a boxcar and flipped my vehicle out into the field. Everything—my pickup, tractor, trailer and tools—was destroyed."

The man struggled for a moment to go on.

"A police officer who 'just happened' to be on the other side of the tracks heard the squeal and crash and came running as soon as he could get across. He was astonished to see me step out of the truck. 'Should you be walking around?' he asked in amazement. He could not believe I had survived. Here was a mangled truck and debris scattered everywhere, and I walked away *without a scratch!*

"Later they found the mangled chainsaw a quarter mile down the track. I could have been in that condition, too, but God was watching over me. I know my wife's prayer for favor is the reason I am here today."

That man experienced a firsthand wake-up call about what it meant to have the favor of God on his life. He did not want to risk ever being without favor again—in fact, he wanted *more* of it. No doubt the thought of what could have happened without God's favor and protection made this man want to get in on the day of salvation and the free favors of God for himself! He was extremely grateful that his wife knew how to pray for favor, but that day he realized the need for a personal connection with God and the favor He offers to His children.

Hitting the Favor Switch

So how do we grow in favor as Jesus did and see its full force unleashed in our lives? In the chapters ahead we will look more closely at the answers to those questions and pinpoint the specific actions we can take to "hit the favor switch." We will examine how our expectations and beliefs affect the levels of favor we experience. We also will determine what part our confessions, the words of our mouths, play in releasing—or resisting—the flow of favor.

Along the way, we will glean from the example of others, both scriptural and contemporary. We will follow the stories of some men and women who knew how to cooperate with God and allow the full force of His favor to operate in their lives. We will see how they increased the level of favor they enjoyed and how we can do the same.

Other stories we follow will demonstrate the dangers that sometimes accompany the flow of favor. Pride and deception, for example, can come in like a flood whenever we begin to think that the favor we enjoy results from our own accomplishments. If we pat ourselves on the back because of our own prowess and forget that everything we are is a direct result of God's mercy and grace, we can diminish in favor rather than grow in it. We will look at how to avoid that trap, which is easy to fall into when everything is going our way, and we will also examine some of the other dangers that accompany favor.

God's favor can make all the difference in the world. It can smooth our way through the minor details of daily living and make our day in little ways. It also can make a tremendous difference in the major situations that arise in life—God's favor can turn around the most difficult circumstances to our benefit and His glory.

Experiencing the favor of God starts with salvation, when we receive God's forgiveness, mercy and grace. That is the place where it all begins, but it does not stop there! My prayer for you is that as you read these pages, you will realize—whether for the first time or all over again in new ways—how completely you are surrounded by God's favor. God's favor is toward *you*, and He wants you to experience its full force at work in your life.

2

Favorable Expectations

You may have heard it said that people rise to the level of your expectations. Generally, the saying holds true. If you expect the best from people, somehow it brings out the best in them. Conversely, the maxim "Don't expect too much and you won't be disappointed" also applies. If you expect the worst from people, you often get it. You will go farther—and so will others—when you have favorable expectations and anticipate the best from people.

So it is with favor. Your level of favor rises to your level of expectation. By definition, to *expect* is to "look forward to something." Looking forward expectantly to God's favor is a giant step toward experiencing its greater release in your life.

Expecting the worst can never bring you the same results. Many believers go through life defeated and depressed because that is what they expect. They are not looking forward to the favor of God. They expect to fail; they expect to be the tail and not the head; they expect to be underneath their circumstances and not above them. The Bible says as a man thinks in his heart, so is he, and according to a man's faith let it be done to him (see Proverbs 23:7; Matthew 9:29). Those with *un*favorable expectations think that although God has saved them, life on earth is supposed to be full of defeat—trial, tribulation and testing of every sort to see if they can *endure* to the end. Since they are expecting a miserable life, then that is what they suffer.

We should recognize here that endurance is a good and godly characteristic. It can even increase favor: "But if when you do what is right and suffer for it you patiently endure it, this finds favor with God" (1 Peter 2:20, NASB). We all walk through trials, but God never meant for us to stay in the midst of them. He "always leads us in triumph in Christ" (2 Corinthians 2:14). When we receive God's forgiveness and are born again, we are not beamed right out of this world, yet neither does God intend for us simply to endure a life of suffering until we finally make it into heaven!

Jesus said, "The kingdom of heaven suffers violence, and the violent take it by force" (Matthew 11:12). That means that the place where God is ruling, *where His favor is*, is actively chosen by those who on purpose press in to take hold of it and receive its benefits. That is where endurance works. Faith endures to receive what is promised, while doubt endures to do without. Expecting the favor God has for you is faith.

My family and I were traveling one day, and someone asked the question, "What gives you peace?" Our son Samuel answered, "Knowing who I am in Christ." We all agreed, but my wife added another thought, saying that being in my arms gives her peace. She explained, "Peace comes from the knowledge of favor—knowing that you are loved—just as turmoil and insecurity reign where you feel rejection. Being in your arms gives me peace because I am soaking up your favor, appreciating that you love me and are for me."

It was not always like that for Jeanie. Early in our marriage she did not receive any of that peace from my hugs, even though I held her in my arms the same way and I really did love her. She interpreted my affection at that time as "marital obligation," rather than as an expression of love. Although I meant to be loving, I was not expressing it the way she expected. She was not able to truly enjoy my love for her until the day she decided to receive it.

You cannot enjoy favor from someone whose favor you refuse to receive. Favor given does not mean favor enjoyed. You cannot experience a great relationship with another person or with God without the flow of favor. To benefit from my favor toward her, Jeanie needed to receive it. Her perspective on my heart was wrong, although it was real to her. Her thoughts kept her from receiving and enjoying my love. What a change in our relationship when Jeanie forgave me and chose to receive my love and favor toward her—in whatever form I expressed it! (By the way, I am having fun finding new ways to show my love for her.)

"How wonderful it is to enjoy the benefits of peace and security!" says Jeanie now. "How I wish I had expected, believed and received your love many years earlier in our marriage!" In the same way, God wants us to expect and receive the favor He offers each of us today.

The Christian life is meant to be enjoyed, not just endured. If we are barely making it through each day, then we are not living our Christianity the way God means for us to live it. Yes, there will be difficult moments, but God wants us not only to get to heaven, but also to enjoy the journey with Him. Part of that enjoyment comes from having the full force of His favor in operation. To grow into that, sometimes we have to change our expectations.

Raising Your Expectations

You may be thinking, *Is it right to have such high expectations of God's favor? Can I really expect Him to shower me with blessings after all He has already done?*

You do indeed have the right to raise your expectations regarding God's favor, but not because of arrogance or pride, and not because you deserve it or because He owes it to you. You have the right simply because you are His child, and He wishes above all that you would "prosper in all things and be in health, just as your soul prospers" (3 John 1:2).

You are a three-part being: spirit, soul and body. As your soul prospers, so will the rest of you. Your soul encompasses your mind, will and emotions. With your mind you expect God's favor; with your will you decide to believe His Word about that favor; and with your emotions you give thanks and rejoice in that favor. When you fill your soul with favorable expectations, you move the heart of God to pour out His favor on your life.

How do we fill ourselves with favorable expectations so that our souls prosper? We already wage a constant battle in our minds against being programmed by this world. Employers or teachers tell us who we are and what we can or cannot do. The media tell us what we should or should not look like. The credit card companies and merchandisers tell us what we should buy. But the Bible says in Romans 12:2, "Do not be conformed to this world, but be transformed by the renewing of your mind." We will not prosper if our expectations are programmed by the world. We prosper by renewing our minds through the Word of God.

When we see what the Word says about God's favor toward us, we cannot help but raise our expectations. Look again at Jesus' words in Nazareth's synagogue: "He has anointed Me . . . to proclaim the accepted and acceptable year of the Lord" (Luke 4:18–19, AMPLIFIED). Everyone in that synagogue knew exactly what Jesus was talking about when He referred to the "acceptable year of the Lord." In Jewish culture this was a name given to the Year of Jubilee. Every fifty years on the Day of Atonement, the priest would go into the holy place and sprinkle blood on the mercy seat. When he walked out, the silver trumpet would be blown. In the Year of Jubilee at the sound of the trumpet, every slave was set free, every debt was cancelled and every piece of property was returned to its original owner (see Leviticus 25:8–17).

The people shouted and rejoiced when the "trumpet of the Jubilee" sounded, and no wonder they celebrated! Imagine your house being instantly paid for, the property you sold coming back to you or regaining your liberty and that of your family. At the Jubilee, everything was redeemed in the physical sense.

When Jesus referred to the Jubilee, however, He had even more in mind. His declaration went far beyond a physical Jubilee. In essence He was declaring, "By My coming and by My death, burial and resurrection, I am bringing a time of spiritual Jubilee—good news for the poor, freedom for the captives, sight for the blind, delivery for the oppressed and salvation and the free favors of God profusely abounding for all." And He intended the spiritual Jubilee to last much longer than a single year. The entire Church age, or what we call the "dispensation of grace," from Jesus' time until He comes back again, is the "acceptable year of the Lord" of which Jesus spoke. That means today is the day of God's favor toward us.

The Old Testament is full of types and shadows, fore-runners of what lay ahead. Hebrews 10:1 says, "The old system in the law of Moses was only a shadow of the things to come, not the reality of the good things Christ has done for us" (NLT). When a shadow crosses your path, you know the reality itself is near. The blood of bulls and goats atoned for sin temporarily but had to be shed again and again. It was a shadow, whereas the reality it foretold, Jesus' blood, atoned once for all. His blood shed for us positioned us to receive His benefits.

The Year of Jubilee brought temporary physical bless-ings. It, too, was a shadow, whereas the reality it foretold, the time of Christ's appearing, brought permanent spiri-tual blessings—favors in profuse abundance, day after day, free for the asking.

But the Year of Jubilee started only at the sound of the trumpet, another shadowing of sorts. The sound of the trumpet noised abroad began the physical Jubilee. When you give voice to your expectations for favor, you begin something in the spiritual. We will talk specifically about confessing favor with the words you speak in another chapter, but for now check your expectations. The "ac-ceptable year of the Lord," when His free favors profusely abound, starts only at the level of your expectation. You can experience salvation and expect nothing more. Or you can expect a spiritual Jubilee, as Jesus proclaimed, and see the full force of favor unleashed in your life.

Faulty Expectations

Most of us like to know what to expect, but sometimes we form faulty expectations rather than getting the facts. If we do not have an accurate picture of what to expect, we can get off track or be misguided and make mistakes. When Jeanie and I first married, for instance, she did not have an accurate picture of what she could expect from me in the home repairs department. Her father, a fix-it man from way back, was more skillful with tools than anyone I have ever known. He never ran across anything he could not repair or even build himself. He could literally take a tractor apart and put it back together right before your eyes. The knock of a repairman had never been heard at their door, nor had their budget ever felt the effects of a repair bill. Thanks to her father's example, Jeanie assumed all husbands were fix-it men.

Consequently, when Jeanie married me she thought I would be eager to develop my home repair skills. Every birthday and Christmas while other men were unwrapping socks and ties, I began getting tools and do-it-yourself books with ominous-sounding titles like *How to Fix Anything*. But it did not take long for Jeanie to realize she might need to change her expectations.

Shortly after we were married, we went to Mexico as missionaries. The water system is different down there. Huge water tanks sit on the rooftops. These tanks contain hundreds of gallons of water, and the arrangement creates a tremendous amount of water pressure. When we turned on our faucets, watch out! One day our shower started leaking, so Jeanie got out a fix-it book she had given me and read up on faucets. Then she went to the hardware store and bought the washers necessary for the repair. By the time I came home that afternoon from teaching at the Bible college, she had all the tools laid out. The fix-it book lay open to the right page. "Honey," she said, "here's everything you need to fix that leaky faucet."

I loved my new bride. I wanted to take care of her the way her dad had, so I grabbed a screwdriver (I figured I could not go wrong with that) and headed into the shower to make the repair. I was about to reveal, however, that I was—and still am—the most unfix-it person you will ever meet.

I do not know if I misread that fix-it book or if the page just failed to mention it, but somehow I forgot to turn off the water first. I was starting in on the faucet with the screwdriver when—*voom!*—that faucet handle shot past me and banged an ugly dent in the back wall. Water started shooting everywhere—you have never seen so much water in your life! With all that pressure behind it, water was spraying like a fire hose all over the place. I stood there with the screwdriver dangling from my hand and tried to stay sanctified.

To this day it is all I can do to walk into a Home Depot without getting the jitters. I just do not fix things, and on top of that, gadgets around the house seem to break whenever they see me coming. But thankfully, Jeanie no longer mistakes me for a repairman. Instead she knows she can expect me to happily pay for one. When something breaks, she gets out the yellow pages and I get out my wallet. On the rare occasions when I do visit Home Depot, I first pray what has become one of my most fervent prayers: *Lord, help me to survive the hardware store!* As soon as I walk in, a man in an orange vest comes up and asks, "Sir, how can I help you?" I tell him what needs fixing, and he knows exactly what the job requires. He gathers the supplies for me, and I think, *Thank You, Lord, for favor!* Then I take everything home for Jeanie to use.

If Jeanie had held on to her faulty expectations about my fix-it abilities, she would have continued to be disappointed in me—not to mention putting some major stress on our marriage. Blinded by frustration, she might not have appreciated the good qualities I do have to offer. Many people choose to focus on the negative about their spouses and overlook the good, but Jeanie was willing to adjust her expectations and enjoy the positive traits she can now see in me—such as my willingness to pay for a handyman.

Likewise, when we have faulty expectations about God we open ourselves up to disappointment and stress. While He continually wants to pour favor on His children, sometimes we do not expect it. If we do not get the facts and form an accurate picture of what He has for us, we are the ones who miss out. Some people figure that whatever God wants to happen in their lives will automatically happen. Instead of expecting what God's Word tells them is theirs, they think, *Whatever God wants me to have will just come my way, and whatever God does not want me to have, I will not receive. It is not up to me, and there is not much I can do about it.*

That kind of thinking is badly mistaken. God told the children of Israel that He had given them the Promised Land, a land flowing with milk and honey. It was theirs for the taking. He had long ago promised it to Abraham, Isaac, Jacob and their descendants, and now Moses and the Israelites stood on the border. God said, "Take possession of the land and live in it, for I have given the land to you to possess" (Numbers 33:53, NASB).

Remember what happened next? Moses sent twelve spies into the land, and the Israelites listened to the ten who brought back a bad report. The people decided that they could not expect to march in and possess a land filled with milk, honey and *giants*. "We were like grasshoppers in our own sight, and so we were in their sight," agreed all the spies save two, so "all the congregation lifted up their voices and cried, and the people wept that night" (Numbers 13:33–14:1).

Did God want the Israelites to enjoy the Promised Land? Absolutely. He assured them it was theirs for the taking. Did they expect things to work out that way? Not at all. They all expected to be killed if they set foot over the border. They could have gone where God wanted them to go, but their faulty expectations took them way off track, and so a whole generation wandered and died in the desert.

Does God want you and me to enjoy the full force of His favor in our lives? Absolutely. Do our expectations enable Him to release that favor on us? Or do we turn off the flow, as the Israelites did? You and I can either stand on the border and entertain faulty expectations that keep us from enjoying our promised land, or we can go in and take possession of the favor God has already assured us is ours.

Knowing What to Expect

In the Old Testament, particularly in the first several books, God often sent people dreams in order to change their expectations. Through a dream, He would let someone know exactly what to expect. God can still use dreams that way, but today we also have His Word to help us form our expectations. His Word helps us raise our expectations so that we can live within the full force of His favor. Consider Joshua 1:8:

> This Book of the Law shall not depart from your mouth, but you shall meditate in it day and night, that you may observe to do according to all that is written in it. For then you will make your way prosperous, and then you will have good success.

Notice that when you meditate in the Word and do as it says, *you* will make your way prosperous. Although God's blessing already awaits you, what you do also makes a difference. If you connect to the presence of God, discover all His Word has to say about favor and live according to that Word, you will have good success!

When you receive with meekness the engrafted Word, says James 1:21, it saves your soul, or mind. You stop thinking the way the world thinks and start thinking the way God thinks about favor.

We will only scratch the surface here, but let's examine a few key Scriptures about favor so we will know what to expect. Consider this portion of Psalm 103:

> Bless the LORD, O my soul,
>   And forget not all His benefits:
> Who forgives all your iniquities,
>   Who heals all your diseases,
> Who redeems your life from destruction,
>   Who crowns you with lovingkindness and tender
>   mercies,
> Who satisfies your mouth with good things,
>   So that your youth is renewed like the eagle's.
> The LORD executes righteousness
>   And justice for all who are oppressed. . . .
> The mercy of the LORD is from everlasting to
>   everlasting
>   On those who fear Him,
>   And His righteousness to children's children,
> To such as keep His covenant.
>
> verses 2–6, 17–18

Just seven verses of a single psalm list a myriad of favorable expectations. The effects of God's favor include forgiving your sins, healing your diseases, redeeming you from hell, heaping goodness and mercy on your head, providing all you need for physical health and strength, giving you justice if you are oppressed, extending His mercy to you forever and His salvation to your children's children when you keep His covenant. And that is just for starters.

Elsewhere Scripture says that in addition to eternal life, God's favor provides you with special talents and abilities, an abundance of the things you need, authority in Jesus' name, deliverance, a healthy mind and body, joy unspeakable, success for your endeavors, protection under His wing, restoration, victory over the enemy, wisdom for the asking and peace past all understanding. God's Word is filled with ways His favor surrounds you like a shield. Whether you go backward, forward, left or right, you can expect to run into God's favor. In fact, you can expect favor to run into *you*. You cannot escape it: "Blessings shall come upon you and overtake you, because you obey the voice of the Lord your God" (Deuteronomy 28:2).

What blessings? As a son or daughter of God the Father, Creator of the vast and priceless universe, you enjoy countless special advantages:

> You will be blessed in your towns and in the country.
> You will be blessed with many children and productive fields.
> You will be blessed with fertile herds and flocks.
> You will be blessed with baskets overflowing with fruit, and with kneading bowls filled with bread.
> You will be blessed wherever you go, both in coming and in going.
> The Lord will conquer your enemies when they attack you. They will attack you from one direction, but they will scatter from you in seven!
> The Lord will bless everything you do and will fill your storehouses with grain.
>
> Deuteronomy 28:3–8, NLT

If you were a child of Bill and Melinda Gates and your father owned Microsoft and was worth some seventy billion dollars, you would enjoy some special advantages and preferential treatment. Doors would be open to you that were not open to just anyone, and you would run into nepotism everywhere you went because of who you were.

Likewise, right now doors are open to you that are open to no one except God's children. His free favors are supposed to profusely abound in your life. If you are not experiencing that kind of abundance, it is time to adopt more favorable expectations. Align yourself with what the Word says about favor, and you will grow in favor. Expect it!

3

Believe Favor Is for You

Many Christians can take the initial step of expecting that God will release favor on His children, especially once they consider what Scripture reveals about His favor, as we did in the last chapter. They understand that God loves His children and wants to bless them with special advantages. It is more difficult for many Christians, however, to take the next step: to believe that God's favor is meant for them *personally*. They see those "special advantages" as being directed to "special people," not to themselves.

Believing that only "special people" can expect God's full favor and that you are not among the special ones will stunt your spiritual growth. (And, of course, if you think you *are* something special compared to the rest of His children, then that will stunt your growth also!)

One definition of *believe* is "to accept as true, genuine or real." Most Christians have no trouble *believing in* God's favor and accepting it as real. For them it is a genuine theological concept—but that is all it is to them. *Believing for* God's favor to be unleashed in their lives personally seems to be a much harder step. Somehow they do not expect God's favor for themselves. There is a world of difference between *believing in* and *believing for* favor.

Every child of God is special, but I meet many who simply do not believe they are part of some select group that is supposed to receive the full force of His favor. They see themselves on the outside of God's blessings and feel unworthy and insignificant. Although they are saved, they believe that until they get to heaven they will only barely get by, only just hang on. They display attitudes such as, "I've always been poor; nobody in my family has ever been rich; I'll never have much. My family has a history of sickness and disease; my brother, aunt and cousin all have mental illness; it's in my genes. Nothing good ever happens to me; nobody ever wants to help me. Nobody likes me; everybody hates me; I'm going to go eat worms. . . ."

Do you remember the Old Testament story of how Job was attacked by the devil? Job's three friends tried to convince Job that God was mad at him. One of them, Bildad, tried to sell Job an inaccurate and "religious" picture of his worthlessness: "If even the moon does not shine, and the stars are not pure in His sight, how much less man, who is a maggot, and a son of man, who is a worm?" (Job 25:5–6).

Jeanie and I once worshiped with a whole church that echoed Bildad. They sang a song I flatly refused to sing. All around me the people sang, "I'm a worm, I'm a worm, I'm a maggot in the dust," so I quoted 2 Corinthians 5:21 to myself instead: "For He made Him who knew no sin to be sin for us, that we might become the righteousness of God in Him." After that song was finished, I saw defeat and depression on the faces all around me. That hymn definitely was not the kind that built faith! But religion can be a mean—and demeaning—thing.

Religion is man trying to reach God, whereas Christianity is just the opposite—it is man responding to God's reaching out. Christians simply respond to what God has already graciously done to reach them. A religious person, however, is trying to reach God through some man-made group of rules and regulations. When you become religious, you know from the start that you probably will not succeed very well in satisfying God—because religion tells you that you are "a worm, a worm, a maggot in the dust." And unless you measure up to the man-made standards and meet the requirements correctly, you go downhill from there. Religion tells you that God is angry with you and is unwilling to bless you, use you or answer your prayers. Furthermore, it tells you He is up in heaven ready to squash you like a bug when you make a wrong move.

Then there is the devil, who tells you the same thing as religion. The devil has a counterfeit for whatever God does. The Spirit of God works by convicting you. You hear in your heart: "God loves you. God is waiting for you with open arms. You need to repent and come to God." The devil counterfeits conviction by working through condemnation. From the devil you hear: "I can't believe you think you're a Christian! Remember what you did? God will be mad at you for a long, long time. He ought to crush you right now. Forget God using you for anything, answering your prayers or blessing you—the favor of God is not for the likes of you!"

I remember another church I visited once where the focus was condemnation, not conviction. I was not yet saved, but my date (a girl I knew before I met Jeanie) asked me to attend church with her, so I gave it a try. The minister stood up front and said something, and then the congregation replied, "I'm a sinner." Then the minister said something else, and again everyone replied, "I'm a sinner." This went on a minimum of fifty times: "I'm a sinner; I'm a sinner; I'm a sinner. . . ."

When I left that church, I felt like a sinner! The devil's condemnation did not connect me to God—it made me want to disconnect. Later, when I got saved, the Spirit's conviction did just the opposite: "You're forgiven; you're forgiven; you're forgiven. . . ." It assured me, "There is therefore now no condemnation to those who are in Christ Jesus, who do not walk according to the flesh, but according to the Spirit" (Romans 8:1).

If you walk according to the flesh and believe the condemnation you hear, between religion and the devil you can end up feeling completely worthless. And if you go around thinking you are a worm and feeling lower than a snake's belly about your place in the Kingdom, you will have a hard time taking the step of believing favor is meant *for you* personally. True, Romans 12:3 warns against thinking more highly of yourself than you ought, and Philippians 2:3 says humbly prefer others before yourself, but those verses do not mean that you must have low self-esteem in order to esteem others.

Note James 2:1, which warns, "My brethren, do not hold the faith of our Lord Jesus Christ, the Lord of glory, with partiality." James even says in verse 9, "If you show partiality, you commit sin." I think James' words apply to dealing with yourself as well as dealing with others. Along with not judging the worth of others, do not judge yourself as inferior or insignificant in the Kingdom of God. You do not need to be in some spiritually select group, be in the ministry or be anything but a child of God to enjoy the full force of God's favor. It is *for you*.

Not for Pastors Only

I recently told the story of my youngest child, Stephanie, who upon graduation from high school told me she wanted to apply to Hillsong in Australia. Stephanie loves to lead praise and worship, and the call of God is on her life. Hillsong has a fantastic Bible college that is an extension of one of the premiere praise and worship churches in the world.

My first response was, "No, you are not going to get on a plane and fly far away to Australia for two years." At seventeen, Stephi was my baby and my only daughter, so I did not even pray about her request. I wanted her to stay home. "We have good colleges right here. Stay home and we will pay your tuition. We will even buy you a car and pay the insurance. We will buy gas to get you to classes, and you can live here for free!"

"Thank you, Dad," Stephanie said gratefully. "But what if God wants me to go somewhere else?"

"Then I guess He will have to buy your car and pay your tuition!" I responded.

We laughed about that, but God was working on me. Before long I also knew Stephi belonged at Hillsong. "Okay, go ahead and apply," I told her.

She sent in her application, only to discover that classes would start before she turned eighteen. Immigration laws require an Australian resident to sign as a minor's guardian in such a case, and we did not know anyone there who could do that for her. As a result, the school told Stephi she would not be able to come.

Letting a policy like that stop us from having to take her to the airport would have been fine with me, except that now I was convinced God wanted her to go. We kept praying about it, and then I called the school.

"She's seventeen—she can't come because of the immigration policy," the voice across the ocean reiterated.

"But we feel like she is supposed to come now. Is there someone else I could talk to?" I asked.

"Here's a supervisor's phone number," the person said.

I called the man and went through our story again.

"In order for your daughter to come," the supervisor said, "you know she would have to have an Australian resident agree to be responsible for her because she's a minor." Then he added, "But I'll do that for you. I'll be her guardian so she can come."

That supervisor went far beyond the call of duty to give us preferential treatment. I am convinced the favor of God opened that door for Stephi to follow the direction God had put in her heart.

Someone who heard me tell that story said, "Well, that just happened for you because you're a pastor." According to this person, being in the ministry entitled me and my family to special favors from God that other Christians cannot enjoy. This person was absolutely convinced that you have to be a pastor or be in the ministry to live in the full favor of God. Nothing could be further from the truth. I know some pastors' families for whom that same door did not open, but it opened for Stephi because we believed God for favor.

One Day of Favor

You, too, need to believe the favor of God will open doors for you that are otherwise closed. You may have heard it said before: It is not a matter of *who* you are; it is a matter of *whose* you are. Position and influence may be contributing factors in gaining the favor of men, but they have nothing to do with the favor of God. Think about how Joseph's favor with men went up and down like a roller coaster (see Genesis 37; 39–40).

Joseph was the favorite of his father but was definitely out of favor with his brothers. They beat him and sold him into slavery—after they decided against actually killing him. The traders who bought him had no use for him either and auctioned him off in Egypt. There he grew in favor with his new master, Potiphar, and wound up having charge of Potiphar's whole estate. But that lasted only until Potiphar's wife falsely accused Joseph of attacking her. Then Potiphar threw him in Pharaoh's dungeon and threw away the key. Joseph's life could have been over as he wasted away in the dungeon, but instead he grew in the favor of his jailer. Through a series of amazing events, he eventually enjoyed the favor of Pharaoh himself and became the prime minister of Egypt.

Do you notice a pattern to Joseph's wild ride? Every time he rose in favor, he did it from the *bottom* of the social ladder. Whereas in Old Testament times a father tended to favor his eldest and heir, Joseph was the eleventh of twelve brothers. Yet he was the favorite son of Jacob. As a new, untried slave, Joseph dragged his chains up on an auction block in Egypt. From that inglorious position he rose to oversee everything Potiphar owned. Then Joseph hit bottom—no place in the world was lower than Pharaoh's dungeon—and from the bottom up he first ran the jail, then ran the whole country!

No matter how low anyone put Joseph, and no matter how often, he just kept rising to the top. How? It obviously had nothing to do with his position or influence, of which he often had neither. I believe Joseph kept rising to the top because the full force of God's favor was at work in his life. "If God is for us, who can be against us?" (Romans 8:31).

I have heard it said that one day of favor is better than a thousand days of labor. In one day of favor you can obtain what someone else might spend his entire life pursuing in vain. During Joseph's time, no doubt there were powerful and influential men who had dreamed their whole lives of becoming prime minister of Egypt. They put everything they had personally, socially and financially into that goal, and they probably were jockeying for position even as Pharaoh had that infamous troubling dream. No one could interpret it for him, and that is when Joseph entered the scene. One of Pharaoh's servants, an ex-prisoner, remembered Joseph, who had been in prison for years and seemed likely to die there. Joseph was summoned, and he interpreted Pharaoh's dream. Then he told Pharaoh what to do about the events the dream foretold and gave the glory to God for his interpretive abilities. You know the rest—God gave Joseph favor with Pharaoh, and right then and there he was promoted from prisoner to prime minister. In one day Joseph obtained the position other people had spent a lifetime coveting in vain.

One day of favor gave Joseph what a thousand days of labor could not! We know how it happened, but what about why? Why did the force of favor both with God and with men flood Joseph's life everywhere he went? In a word, Joseph believed. In every change of circumstance, Joseph kept believing God was *for him*. He kept living out and confessing his faith. He told Potiphar's seductive wife he could never commit such a sin against God; he told Pharaoh it was God who enabled him to interpret dreams; he told his brothers what they had meant for evil in his life God had meant for good (see Genesis 39:9; 41:16; 50:20). Despite every injustice perpetrated against him, he held anger and bitterness at bay, and he held an unshakeable conviction that God could turn around any situation, as long as Joseph followed Him.

Sin and Failure Cannot Stop Favor

Maybe you are thinking, *That may have worked for Joseph, but it won't work for me. Joseph kept following God, but I have made so many mistakes, done so many things wrong. I have made a huge mess of my life! I can't believe God would send good things my way.*

It is vital to understand that sin and failure cannot knock you out of the path of favor—but unbelief can. Sin cannot keep you away from God. Why? Because God is not holding your sins against you. He has blotted them out: "For God was in Christ, reconciling the world to himself, no longer counting people's sins against them" (2 Corinthians 5:19, NLT). No matter what you did or what was done to you in your past, no matter how much the devil has tried to steal from, kill and destroy you, when you experience salvation, you are a completely new creation: "What this means is that those who become Christians become new persons. They are not the same anymore, for the old life is gone. A new life has begun!" (2 Corinthians 5:17, NLT).

If God does not introduce you to yourself through His Word after you are saved, you will not know who you are. We all need to know *who* the Word says we are and *whose* it says we are.

If God could not use anyone with past failures and character flaws, the Bible would be practically bereft of stories. Think about the people God has had working for Him: Peter denied the Lord not once but three times, after vehemently telling Jesus he would never do so. Mighty King David, the man after God's own heart, committed adultery and then murdered the woman's husband. Before he was an apostle, Paul helped with the stoning of Stephen and mercilessly persecuted the early believers. The prophet Jeremiah got so discouraged that he felt like quitting the ministry and opening an inn for travelers in the desert. Elijah ran from Queen Jezebel in fear. Abraham compromised with his wife's servant, Hagar. Isaac lied that his wife was his sister. Jacob was called a deceiver. Lot, albeit a righteous man, made his home in Sodom. Yet God used these people who turned to Him in faith.

If that does not yet convince you that God can use you, the list goes on: Noah got drunk. Samson was a womanizer. Rahab had been a prostitute. Jonah ran away from God. Zechariah did not believe the angel who told him he would have a son. The disciples fell asleep when Jesus asked them to pray. Martha worried too much. Thomas was a doubter. Timothy had stomach trouble. Zacchaeus was too short. Everyone but Jesus had faults and flaws.

When you repent of past failures, God puts them behind you for good. "He is faithful and just to forgive us our sins and to cleanse us from all unrighteousness" (1 John 1:9). How long does it take until you are worthy to be favored and used again? Forgiveness is instantaneous. As I mentioned earlier, the devil works through condemnation and will have you believing you need to suffer and beg. If you listen to him, three or four days later you will be going back to God to repent again: "Oh, God, remember what I did? Forgive me! I need to ask again, to make sure, to say how sorry I am. . . ."

Expressing heartfelt repentance is one thing, but going back over and over again to beg God to forgive you is another thing—it is unbelief. God forgave you *and* forgot your sin the first time you asked. When you go back to Him to beg again and again, I can imagine God up in heaven saying to Gabriel, "What is this child talking about? I have no idea. I do not remember anything. Pull his file—the way he is acting, he must have done *something*."

Gabriel gets on the computer and pulls up your name and file. God asks, "Well, what did he do? What do you have on him?"

Gabriel replies, "The file says he is washed in the blood. He is a joint heir with Christ and an ambassador for Your Kingdom. It says here we are building him a mansion on the corner of Glory Avenue and Hallelujah Street. I don't see any problem. We've got nothing on him!"

When you repent, you receive immediate forgiveness and you are justified. Jesus was "delivered up because of our offenses, and was raised because of our justification" (Romans 4:25). To be *justified* is to be made *just-as-if-I'd* never done it. That is how God sees you once you ask forgiveness—just as if you had never sinned.

You may be in a bad spot in life because of sin or failure, but that is one of the most crucial times to believe for favor! When your house is the darkest, it is still wired for electricity. You just need to hit the switch to turn on the light. When you are in a dark spot personally, God's favor is still available to you. You just need to connect with it by believing.

Job was in the middle of the trial of his life when he said, "You have granted me life and favor, and Your care has preserved my spirit" (Job 10:12). Job had lost his family, his possessions and his health, yet in the midst of horrendous loss he believed for God's favor. Note that even though the book of Job is 42 chapters long, it did not take 42 years for Job to see results. Most Bible scholars agree that the entire saga of Job transpired in three to nine months. By the end of that time, "the LORD turned the captivity of Job" and "gave Job twice as much as he had before" (Job 42:10, KJV).

When Job was in his darkest time, God turned his situation around with favor. The same can be true for you. God wants to give you double for your trouble, as He did for Job. Your past history and your sins covered under Jesus' blood can never separate you from God's favor. Unbelief does that. Turn on the favor by believing for it, as Job did!

Believing Is Seeing

People have told me, "That sounds great, but I never see it. I believe in God, pray and go to church, but I just never experience that kind of favor."

Why don't they experience it? They believe *in* it, but they are not believing *for* it. They either do not know they can expect it, as we talked about in chapter 2, or they expect it for God's "special" children but not for themselves, as we talked about earlier in this chapter. You do not receive what you are ignorant of, and you do not receive what you are not believing for.

The attitude of "I'll believe it when I see it—God knows where I live, and if He wants to bless me, He can find me" does not put you on the receiving end of God's favor either. The Kingdom does not work that way. Everything in the Kingdom comes to you by faith. You do not get saved because you need salvation—everybody needs salvation. You get saved because you believe. You do not get healed because you need healing—countless people need healing. You get healed because you believe for it. You do not get delivered because you need deliverance—so do many others. You get delivered when you believe for deliverance. The same is true of God's favor. You will see the supernatural favor of God manifest in your life when you believe for His supernatural favor.

If your relationship with your earthly father was less than it should have been, you may have trouble accepting that God looks on you with favor. Many people equate God the Father's character with that of their earthly fathers. If your earthly father was unloving, distant or absent, you may think of your heavenly Father that way. If you grew up under a harsh disciplinarian, you may envision God as a big bully or a stern judge just waiting for you to step out of line. And when you do—*zap*—He will nail you with a bolt of lightning.

Often people believe that the negative, disappointing and devastating things they experience are punishments or judgments from God. That is not at all His plan for you. Favor is His plan. It was God the Father's idea to reconcile the world to Himself and not count your sins against you. James 1:16–17 tells us, "Do not be deceived, my beloved brethren. Every good gift and every perfect gift is from above, and comes down from the Father of lights, with whom there is no variation or shadow of turning."

In Scripture, whenever God says, "Do not be deceived," He is forewarning us about an area where most Christians easily fall prey to deception. In this passage in James, He makes it clear that He is the source of *good* gifts and that He does not change. Verse 18 goes on to say, "In his goodness he chose to make us his own children by giving us his true word. And we, out of all creation, became his choice possession" (NLT). Out of all creation we became—*you* became—His choice possession. You were made but a little lower than the angels and crowned with glory and favor (see Psalm 8:5).

That's who the Word of God says you are, so let it introduce you to yourself. Let it transform your mind to believe that His favor rests on you. That is His will for your life. Your part is to believe it.

"Do you believe that I am able to do this?" Jesus asked two blind men crying out to Him for the restoration of their sight. When they answered, "Yes, Lord," Jesus replied, "It shall be done to you according to your faith," (Matthew 9:28–29, NASB).

4

Faith Will Move Your Mouth

When the great evangelist Smith Wigglesworth was more than eighty years old, someone asked him, "Smith, do you ever have any bad days? How do you feel?"

Smith's reply was instantaneous. "I never ask Smith how I feel," he told the inquirer. "I tell him how he feels."

No wonder Smith Wigglesworth was able to minister well into his eighties and have his ministry marked by so many healings and miracles. He knew that "death and life are in the power of the tongue, and those who love it will eat its fruit" (Proverbs 18:21). He regularly ate the fruit of his faith-filled words.

What about you and me? What kind of diet do we put ourselves on spiritually with our words? We all need to listen to ourselves because what we are saying makes a tremendous difference in our lives. What are you saying about your family, your future, your health, your finances or the favor of God in your life? It would do us all good to carry around a tape recorder and then play it back at the end of the day. We probably would be shocked at our own words.

Personally, I do not need a tape recorder to play back my words. My wife, Jeanie, and I agreed early in our relationship to help each other watch our words. It is a good thing she helps me in this area—I need her help much more than she needs mine. She makes sure I watch what I say. For example, through the years we have graphed our church's growth. January attendance is good; February is better. March is terrific, and by April attendance is phenomenal. Then about the second week of May, people who are not strongly committed end up going golfing on sunny Sundays or enjoying a day at the lake. Attendance has been known to taper off a bit—sometimes even nosedive on really beautiful weekends. One spring I said to Jeanie, "It's that time again. We need to get ready for the summer slump."

"Is that what you want to see this year?" she asked. "Is that what you are believing God for? Maybe you ought to listen to some of those sermon tapes by that one pastor, Duane Vander Klok. He preached some great messages on Isaiah 57:19, the verse where God says, 'I create the fruit of the lips.'"

Ouch. Jeanie was right. I needed to take my words in a positive direction. I cannot overemphasize the importance of our words. Expecting favor and believing for favor are both giant steps toward seeing favor unleashed, but the next step, confessing God's favor with the words of our mouths, is absolutely essential.

Speaking Is Believing

If you have faith for something, if you believe for it, do you know what happens? You begin to speak it out. That spirit of faith deep inside of you rises up and overflows in your words. "Out of the abundance of the heart the mouth speaks," Jesus said (Matthew 12:34). He also told His disciples, "Assuredly, I say to you, if you have faith as a mustard seed, you will say to this mountain, 'Move from here to there,' and it will move; and nothing will be impossible for you" (Matthew 17:20).

If you have faith . . . you will *say*. You will *speak*. But most of us do not *talk to* our mountains as Jesus instructed. We *talk about* them: "I have dealt with this problem for twenty years; my problem is so big; my problem has cost me a fortune. . . ." Jesus said to speak to our mountains, not about them. What do we say? We tell them to be removed and cast into the sea.

People have told me, "Maybe God wants this problem in my life for a reason. Maybe I am supposed to learn something."

"Listen," I always reply, "if God wanted that mountain in your life, He would not have told you how to get rid of it!"

Do not accept a long-term problem as a permanent part of your life just because that is the way you have always been. Do you have a problem with anger? Speak to that problem: "I am delivered from anger in Jesus' name." Pornography? "I am delivered from pornography in Jesus' name. Greater is He that is in me than he that is in the world" (see 1 John 4:4). Whatever your problem, release your faith through your words to move that mountain.

I heard a true story about a woman who knew how to do just that. A certain problem in her life looked like a mountain to her. She had smoked cigarettes for years and wanted to quit, but she just could not. She tried and tried without result. Then she heard that Proverbs 18:21 says death and life are in the power of the tongue. She decided to speak to her mountain and tell it to be removed. The first thing she did every morning when she got up was light a cigarette. But as she lit up, she started saying, "I am delivered from tobacco in Jesus' name. My body does not even like tobacco; my body is repulsed by it." Then she would smoke her cigarette. She lit up a number of times during the day, but every time, she would say the same thing as she puffed away: "I am delivered from this in Jesus' name. My body hates this tobacco. I hate it."

The woman kept this up for some time. One morning she got up and lit up but noticed that the cigarette did not taste right. Smoking it made her nauseous, and afterward she vomited. Later in the day, she lit up again as usual, and as usual she declared, "I am delivered from tobacco in Jesus' name. My body is repulsed by it." Sure enough, again smoking nauseated her and again she got sick to her stomach. From then on she had no desire to smoke! God had empowered her tongue with life and death—life to her health and death to her long-term smoking habit. She expected the proverb from God's Word to work, she believed it would work for her and she kept confessing it daily, even hourly, until she realized its full benefits and could rejoice that she was free.

Scripture is rich with principles about speaking out what you believe. Romans 10:8 says, "'The word is near you, in your mouth and in your heart' (that is, the word of faith which we preach)." Notice your word of faith is not in just one place or the other. If it is only in your heart or only in your mouth, it will not work.

What must happen for faith to work? It must be in both places. If your faith will not move your mouth, it will not move mountains or anything else, either! Look at the next verse, Romans 10:9, which talks about salvation: "If you confess with your mouth the Lord Jesus and believe in your heart that God has raised Him from the dead, you will be saved."

Remember that I said everything in the Kingdom of God works the same way? God has ordained spiritual laws that do not change. For salvation you both confessed and believed. Colossians 2:6 says, "As you therefore have received Christ Jesus the Lord, so walk in Him." We walk out our Christian lives in the same way we received salvation—by confessing and believing. Favor follows this principle. When your faith for favor is both in your heart *and* in your mouth, you will experience favor in incredible ways.

Christians who do not speak out the favor of God on their lives cannot experience its full effects. They may live for God, they may pray and read the Bible and go to church, but they will not see supernatural favor because they are not declaring it. It is as if they are holding a loaded gun but are not pulling the trigger. Nothing happens; the gun is useless. To fire a gun you must pull the trigger.

To see the full force of God's favor unleashed, you must confess the belief in your heart. You have to get up in the morning 365 days a year and let your faith move your mouth. Both Old and New Testament writers attested to the necessity of declaring what you believe. The apostle Paul wrote, "And since we have the same spirit of faith, according to what is written, 'I believed and therefore I spoke,' [Psalm 116:10] we also believe and therefore speak" (2 Corinthians 4:13). In the Old Testament, consider Job 22:28: "You will also declare a thing, and it will be established for you." The same verse in the AMPLIFIED goes on to say, "and the light [of God's favor] shall shine upon your ways." That is a one-verse summary of my point—when you confess the favor for which you are expecting and believing, God establishes it and shines the light of His favor all over you.

Unleash your faith—and the force of favor—through your words. At the start of the day, pray: "God, I thank

You that Your favor surrounds me like a shield today. I thank You that doors are going to open for me that would otherwise be closed and that people will want to help me. As I choose to walk in Your ways, even my enemies will be at peace with me today because You are so good and because this is the day that Your free favors will abound in my life."

Confessing *God's* Word, Not Your Own

Instances have occurred where people have taken the idea of confessing for things by faith to extremes. People have confessed for all kinds of things, but I believe that to avoid extremes in this area, you and I need to acknowledge that we are to be submitted to God—He is not forced to submit to our words. We cannot order God around or tell Him what to do, and He cannot be manipulated by us. That is unscriptural.

As Scripture says, however, God scrupulously keeps His own Word: "I am watching over My word to perform it" (Jeremiah 1:12, NASB). The key to biblical confession, then, is to make sure we are confessing *God's* Word, not our own.

To *confess* means to "admit or profess." When you confess faith for something, you are admitting or professing that you agree with God about it. You say the same thing as God's Word, to which He is faithful. You cannot name and claim just anything and everything that comes to mind. You cannot go around saying "I am going to have 78 oil wells" and expect God to give you 78 oil wells. God does not promise you oil wells in His Word, so you are not speaking in agreement with Him.

As His child, however, you can claim by naming or agreeing with any promise God gives in His Word and expect that He will keep it—in fact, that is what you are supposed to do. That is the whole idea behind letting your faith move your mouth. Find out what His Word promises and speak those promises over your life. God says you are surrounded by favor, so believe and confess for it. He says by Jesus' stripes you were healed, so speak out that promise for your physical healing. He says if you follow Him, even your enemies will be at peace with you, so expect to enjoy favor with both God and men. Speaking in agreement with God's Word is biblical confession, and it releases your faith in what God said He is going to do. "No matter how many promises God has made, they are 'Yes' in Christ" (2 Corinthians 1:20, NIV).

Some people may be resistant to formulas, especially formulas they have tried and perhaps misapplied without seeing the hoped-for results. But expecting, believing and confessing for favor (or God's other promises) in agreement with the Word is not a formula, and we will talk more about that in the next chapter.

Faith is not a matter of simply doing steps 1, 2 and 3 and getting 4 on demand, nor can you manipulate God to fulfill your every whim. Yet salvation and the spiritual laws of the Kingdom do operate with a wonderful simplicity that God has ordained. "It is impossible for God to lie," says Hebrews 6:18, and when God ordains something, we can be sure He will carry it through. When He says in Isaiah 57:19, "I create the fruit of the lips," we need to take Him at His Word and start watching what we say. Our words are containers, so to speak, that release seeds of faith from our hearts. God causes those seeds to bear fruit. That begs the question: What kind of seeds are we planting? Since death and life are in the power of our tongues and God creates the fruit of our lips, we would do well to make sure the words coming out of our mouths bear not rotten fruit but good fruit.

Eating Our Words

Has anyone ever told you, "Be careful what you say—you may have to eat your words"? If you have ever uttered words you should not have said, you know the "bad taste" they can leave in your mouth.

How do your words taste? I want to make sure my words are sweet because, in reality, I am going to "eat all my words" and reap their results as God creates the fruit of my lips. With our words we can plant faith seeds for good things, as Smith Wigglesworth did regarding his health, or faith seeds for bad things. Whatever is inside our hearts comes out in our words. Jesus told us it would—"A good man out of the good treasure of his heart brings forth good things, and an evil man out of the evil treasure brings forth evil things" (Matthew 12:35).

If evil things come out of a person's mouth, what kind of fruit can he or she expect to reap? People who spout constantly negative news soon find depression wrapped around their souls. People who say, "I am always the first to be laid off; I will probably go broke and my house will be repossessed" soon find financial trouble at their door (especially if their employer lays off the whiney workers first). People who complain, "My health since I hit fifty is going straight downhill; I have pains in my back and aches in my knees—in twenty years I will probably need a wheelchair" might as well buy that wheelchair now since they are already talking themselves into it. Negative words release faith for results people do not desire, and even worse, they give Satan license to attempt to bring about those destructive results.

People who speak good news, on the other hand, soon find themselves abundantly blessed as they reap the fruit of their lips. A single mother approached me with a huge smile after one of our services. The job of a single parent can be unbelievably difficult, and discouragement waits around every corner. But this woman had learned to speak in agreement with God's Word and plant good seeds with her words. She told me she had begun to confess daily that she was surrounded by favor. "God is just blessing me!" she reported. "I know His favor is at work—He recently took my income from $15,000 a year to $45,000!"

"You're right, that's the favor of God," I told her. She was declaring it everywhere she went, and I could see it shining all over her. She was walking in victory because she knew how to align her words with God's Word.

Revelation 12:11 lists two things that are necessary to be an overcomer like that: "And they [that's us] overcame him [the devil] by the blood of the Lamb and by the word of their testimony." The blood of the Lamb has already been shed and has defeated the devil—that was God's part. Our part is to make sure our confession, or the word of our testimony, agrees with what Jesus purchased for us.

When we line up our words with what the blood of Jesus purchased for us, we enjoy salvation, healing, deliverance and favor according to the words of our mouths. Rather than picturing ourselves as elderly invalids who are senile and barely able to sit up in wheelchairs, we should picture ourselves with our youth being renewed like the eagle's (see Psalm 103:5). "As your days, so shall your strength be," God said (Deuteronomy 33:25). When I am eighty, I still plan to jog in the morning and have strength left over for the rest of the day, because I am confessing my faith for it all along the way. I am saying, "I am strong in the Lord and in the power of His might; the Lord is my light and my salvation; surely goodness and mercy (that's favor) will follow me all the days of my life, and I will dwell in the house of the Lord forever."

How about you? What are you confessing? Your experiences in life are largely determined by the words of your mouth. You can prepare the way for God to move—or you can hinder His moving—by what you say. Foretelling of John the Baptist, Isaiah said he would be a "voice of one crying in the wilderness: 'Prepare the way of the LORD'" (Isaiah 40:3). Like John, use your voice to prepare the Lord's way. It is like preparing for harvest based on the seeds you sow. Just as you plant cucumber seeds in your garden to reap cucumbers or corn seeds to reap corn, you plant a favorable confession to reap favor. Whatever you plant—physical or spiritual—comes up true to its nature. If you plant seeds of ill health, depression, bitterness or any number of negative things with your words, then that is what you will reap. You cannot have a negative mouth and reap a positive life.

Your spiritual crop will come up true to the nature of the "seeds" you plant. You will have success or defeat, victory or loss based on the words of your mouth. As much as God wants you to enjoy the benefits of His favor, you can choose to deny them with the words of your mouth. Or you can say, "The favor of God is turning my life around every day. I will have success and victory. I am blessed coming and going and every way I turn because His favor surrounds me like a shield." If you will plant seeds for favor, blessings and abundance, those are what you will reap.

Confession and the Domino Effect

Your positive or negative confessions are so powerful that they affect much more than your own life. The words you speak can have a domino effect in the lives of others. Think about some of your most joyous or most painful memories. Often those memories involve something significant that someone said to you. Perhaps a parent or teacher motivated you to reach for an important goal because he or she believed in you and told you so. Or perhaps you were told as a child that you were worthless and would never amount to anything, and you have spent much time and effort recovering from those wounding words. You can greatly encourage—or greatly discourage—others with what you say.

I find it fascinating that the Bible records more than one instance where the power of speech was forbidden or even removed to prevent the domino effect of negative words. Remember the story of the fall of Jericho, when the city's walls fell down flat at the people's shout? There was power in that shout, no doubt, but I believe there was even more power in the silence that preceded it.

Joshua and the Israelites were encamped outside Jericho, and God told Joshua that He had given the city into their hands. The city was securely shut up against them, so things did not look promising for victory. But God had a plan. Joshua and the men of war were to march around the city once a day for six days, along with seven priests bearing seven trumpets before the Ark of the Covenant. On the seventh day they were to march around the city seven times, and at the long blast of a trumpet all the people were to shout a great shout. God said that at the great shout, "The wall of the city will fall down flat. And the people shall go up every man straight before him" (Joshua 6:5).

That seemed an odd way to breach the city walls, and Joshua, being a wise leader, knew there would be some talk about it. He decided to nip any negative talk in the bud: "Now Joshua had commanded the people, saying, 'You shall not shout or make any noise with your voice, *nor shall a word proceed out of your mouth*, until the day I say to you, "Shout!" Then you shall shout'" (Joshua 6:10, italics added).

Why did Joshua insist on absolute silence until the very moment of the shout? He knew that on day one, after doing nothing but marching with the priests around the city and looking at its strong, towering walls, his men of war would start to talk. "This is the dumbest thing I have ever heard of in my life," one might say. "We are going to walk around this wall for seven days, then *shout?* This isn't going to work—except to make our enemies laugh at us."

"Yeah," another might sarcastically agree. "I am sure our marching around and around will frighten their warriors, especially when they see us standing here yelling, doing nothing with our weapons."

"I tell you," a third might insist, "I am not a big enough fool to walk around in circles another day. We should be *doing* something. I say we attack now!"

That kind of talk would have had a domino effect all right, but not on the stones of Jericho's walls! The disobedient Israelites would have fallen man after man as the enemy atop the wall slaughtered them. God's plan to knock the walls flat was much more efficient—albeit unusual. In this case Joshua knew that silence among the soldiers would be golden, at least until the appropriate time for the shout.

Sometimes you just need to zip your lip and say nothing. Negative words have a negative effect on you and on everyone around you. Every child hears the maxim, "If you can't say something nice, don't say anything at all" at least a thousand times. I certainly did. Think about it—such a maxim would not be necessary if there were not power in the spoken word.

Zacharias was another case in Scripture where silence was golden—except he had his lip zipped for him. He was a priest, and the lot had fallen to him to burn incense in the Temple of the Lord. While he was carrying out his duty, the angel Gabriel appeared and said,

FAITH WILL MOVE YOUR MOUTH

"Do not be afraid, Zacharias, for your prayer is heard; and your wife Elizabeth will bear you a son, and you shall call his name John. And you will have joy and gladness, and many will rejoice at his birth. For he will be great in the sight of the Lord."

Luke 1:13–15

That was astonishing news for Zacharias and Elizabeth, who had been childless all their lives. Rather than welcoming the angel's message with joy, though, Zacharias confessed his doubt instead: "Do you expect me to believe this? I'm an old man and my wife is an old woman" (Luke 1:18, MESSAGE).

That reply did not earn Zacharias Gabriel's favor! I can imagine Gabriel thundering back, "I am Gabriel, who stands in the presence of God. . . . Behold, you will be mute and not able to speak until the day these things take place, because you did not believe my words" (Luke 1:19–20).

And so Zacharias' lip was zipped for him. He was granted zero opportunity to spread around his doubt with his words. He remained speechless until the day of John the Baptist's birth.

Zacharias' silence proved golden, I think, because it taught him an important lesson about lining up his confession with the Word of God. When his tongue was loosed, the first words he uttered were positive words of praise to the Lord. Such positive words can have more of a domino effect on people than negative words. Their result is far better, too. Proverbs 15:23 says, "A man has joy by the answer of his mouth, and a word spoken in due season, how good it is!" You can spread joy all around you with your good words.

I have always been grateful that Bernie Blauwkamp, one of my associate pastors, purposefully arranged to have that kind of effect on me. When we first moved

59

into our church building, a little more than 50 percent of all the finances that came in went directly into our building payment. We had built large, and we were not even filling the place up one time a weekend. God had given our church body a vision, and I was confessing God's favor for us, so I was not anxious about our monetary state . . . just a little concerned. From time to time, I would go by the church's accounting office and ask, "How are we doing?"

Bernie noticed my repeated inquiries, so he gave his assistant special instructions about me. "Every time Pastor Duane comes in to ask how we are doing, you smile big and tell him, 'We're doing fantastic. We're loaded!'"

On Mondays I would often stick my head into the accounting office, and his assistant would greet me with a big smile. "How are we doing financially?" I would ask.

"Pastor," she would reply, "we're loaded. We're just loaded!"

I would walk out of there feeling like a million bucks, even though we did not have a million. I do not know about Bernie, but I would face the rest of the week's pastoral responsibilities with my mind at peace about our finances.

Bernie spoke out and declared the financial favor for which he was believing, and he encouraged himself and others in the process. The favor we were confessing has come to pass—that building has long been paid off, and we fill it up many times over every weekend. We balance our budget and run in the black every year, and Bernie is still in charge of our accounting office. And to this day, every time I stick my head in his office to ask for an update, he tells me, "We're loaded, Pastor. We're just loaded!"

5

Favor Is Not a Formula

You do not need a degree in theology to experience the benefits of salvation. Salvation depends
instead on simple, childlike faith. Likewise, favor
is not limited to those who have a great understanding of
the Bible. Anyone can experience God's favor by believing
it is available to him or her and confessing it.

These are simple enough conditions for receiving
God's favor, but no matter how simple the conditions
are, they are not a magic formula whereby you can say
"one, two, three" and—*poof*—you automatically get favor
as a result. Walking in the full benefits of God's favor is
a process for any believer. It takes some maturity. After
all, Jesus Himself *grew* in the favor of God and men.

Growing in favor is a maturation process almost akin
to building your muscles. Your body already has all the
muscles you need. It is quite another matter, however,
to strengthen those muscles to peak performance. Good

muscle tone is not automatic, especially in our somewhat sedentary society; many of us, therefore, content ourselves with flabby muscles that tire out quickly. We could be physically stronger, but we do not exercise because it is plain hard work. Then when we do something a little physically demanding, we wonder how we could be so sore from an hour's exertion!

The same is true with favor. You already are surrounded by all the favor of God you need, but many Christians are content with living at the starting point of favor: salvation. They breathe a sigh of relief to be heading toward heaven but do not press on to work out their salvation. Instead of growing up spiritually, they remain spiritual babies, content to have others feed them the Word and take care of them. Then they wonder why they struggle along in their spiritual walk, while other believers' lives seem to overflow with God's powerful favor.

You have to build your spiritual muscles in order to experience favor working at peak performance in your life. You have to train yourself in the principles of favor and discipline yourself to put them into practice daily.

Daily Labor Unleashes Favor

Long ago, Jeanie and I decided we wanted to stay healthy and strong. God expects us to take good care of our physical bodies so we can carry out all His plans for us. For that reason we implemented an exercise program. Six days a week we work out by jogging, biking, swimming, weight lifting or exercising in some form. We have enjoyed running together for many years now.

Exercising each day is good for my health, but suppose I decide that it is too much trouble to do a little each day. I decide to take the next month off. Then all in one day I decide to "catch up" by running three hundred miles, swimming twenty miles and biking seven hundred miles, plus lifting weights. That exercise would *not* be good for my health!

It is the exercise you do consistently, day after day, that builds your strength. Many areas in life operate the same way. This is especially true regarding your spiritual growth, including your growth into more favor. Momentous events will take place that greatly affect you, but by far the greatest impact on your life comes from the little things you do every day, day after day.

Let me suggest to you five habits that I believe are essential in keeping oneself in position to enjoy the favor that flows from a strong relationship with God. I have chosen to practice these habits daily. They keep me healthy and strong physically, mentally, emotionally and spiritually, and I highly recommend them. They will work for you, too.

I already mentioned one of them: physical exercise six days a week (one day of rest to let your body recuperate is good). Another is making sure I touch my family every day both physically and in other ways, such as emotionally with words of love and encouragement. This keeps our relationships strong and secure. I also rarely miss a daily study hour in which I read books that stretch my mind and my knowledge of the world around me. Education is a lifelong process and should not stop after formal schooling. Daily prayer is another of my vital habits—not the rote recitation of formal prayers but talking directly to the Lord from the heart. And at the top of my list, though I mention it last since I will cover it in detail, is reading the Bible. I put God's Word in my heart every day without fail. From the time I was saved years ago, I decided I would not let a single day pass without reading the Bible, and I have kept my commitment every day since. Joshua 1:8 says,

This Book of the Law shall not depart from your mouth, but you shall meditate in it day and night, that you may observe to do according to all that is written in it. For then you will make your way prosperous, and then you will have good success.

Enjoying God's favor is a large part of being prosperous and having good success, and those things come directly from delving daily into the Word of God. Remember how faith comes? "Faith comes by hearing, and hearing by the word of God" (Romans 10:17). Notice that faith does not come from "having heard," past tense. It is "hearing," present tense—hearing again and again. To build your spiritual muscles and your faith for favor, you need to be hearing the Word of God continually. You cannot read a verse once or ten times or even a hundred times and receive all the revelation God has for you in it. More is always there, and you are changed each time you read it. A message a week at church is not enough, either. You have to put the Word inside you daily.

As you read the Word daily, you will discover that you already have the favor of God. You will know you are meant to live victoriously, filled with peace and with purpose. You will be healed, prosperous and delivered, to name a few of God's benefits toward you. God will introduce you to yourself, to who you are as His child. As you meditate on the Word day and night, it will change what you say—out of the abundance of the heart your mouth speaks (see Luke 6:45).

You can easily tell if you have not meditated enough on the Word. You cannot hide it—your mouth will give you away by speaking words from your heart that do not agree with God's plan. You need a heart full of faith for favor, victory, peace and all the other blessings God says are yours. Building up your faith day after day through the Word takes discipline, as does praying and following the other daily habits I mentioned. But such daily labor will unleash favor. You change your life when you change what you do every day.

Think about what made Daniel in the Old Testament great. Like Joseph, Daniel rose from being a prisoner in a foreign land to being one of the king's most prominent and trusted officials. I believe that what Daniel did every day made him great. The Bible records his daily habits: "And in his upper room, with his windows open toward Jerusalem, he knelt down on his knees three times that day, and prayed and gave thanks before his God, *as was his custom since early days*" (Daniel 6:10, italics added). "That day" was the day Daniel found out the king had signed a life-threatening decree. Anyone who prayed to a god other than the king for the next thirty days would be cast into the lions' den.

Daniel knew how vital his daily habit of prayer was, and he put his life in jeopardy to carry it through and keep his relationship to God alive and connected. He was indeed thrown into the lions' den, but God's angel shut the lions' mouths. Daniel lived, while his accusers took his place in the jaws of the beasts.

Daniel had the favor of both God and the king. Look what the king cried out at the lions' den the morning following Daniel's punishment: "Daniel, servant of the living God, has your God, whom you serve continually, been able to deliver you from the lions?" (Daniel 6:20). Daniel's answer, of course, was yes, but note something else here: Even the highest official in the land had noticed that Daniel was a man who served God *continually*.

From his first day as a prisoner in that land, Daniel had labored daily to honor God by keeping His Word. The first time he was brought into the king's palace, he purposed in his heart that he would not defile himself by eating the king's delicacies and drinking the wine. (Notice Daniel was in the habit of keeping his body healthy and strong. The king's food was not only outside the Mosaic Law, but it also was unhealthy. Imagine what eating cheesecake every day would do to you!) Daniel appealed to the chief eunuch to test the Israelite youths with their own diet of vegetables and water (see Daniel 1:8–21). The chief eunuch consented because "God had brought Daniel *into the favor* and goodwill of the chief of the eunuchs" (verse 9, italics added). The young men's healthy diet paid off. They soon proved themselves to be in better condition than any of the trainees who ate the king's rich fare.

Besides good health, God also favored Daniel and his companions with knowledge and skill in literature and wisdom, and to Daniel He gave the ability to understand dreams and visions. At the end of their training period, the king found the young Israelites "ten times better than all the magicians and astrologers who were in all his realm" (verse 20). Daniel's important daily habits unleashed favor with both God and men. Daniel and his friends were ten times wiser and ten times more advanced than all the other trainees around them. Even the king noticed how they stood out among their peers.

When you practice good habits that promote favor, God can release ten times the wisdom, the health, the skill or whatever you need toward you. Good habits enable favor, and favor enables advancement and success.

Favor-Hindering Habits

Just as you can adopt daily habits that promote favor, you also can adopt daily habits that prevent it. Favor-hindering habits are easy to form because they do not require discipline. If you get into the flesh for just a little while, words come out of your mouth that drive faith and favor far from you. In its natural state, when it is not renewed by God's Word, your mind is at war with God. Romans 8:6–8 warns, "For to be carnally minded is death, but to be spiritually minded is life and peace. Because the carnal mind is enmity against God . . . those who are in the flesh cannot please God."

The natural mind sets itself against the things of the Spirit. If you could see the car from that train wreck we talked about in chapter 1, where the man walked away without a scratch, your carnal mind would try to tell you, "That wasn't really God! It was one of those freak things, a coincidence. It had nothing to do with God's protection or favor—the guy was just plain lucky." Or suppose they rolled a casket down the aisle to the front of your church, and everyone prayed for a man dead three days to live again. Suppose he sat up and climbed out. Do you know what your carnal mind would say? "He wasn't really dead. He was in a deep coma."

The carnal mind has an answer for everything God does. That is why saying the first thing that pops into your head usually gets you into trouble—the things that come to mind naturally are usually dead wrong. "The tongue is a flame of fire," says James 3:6. "It is full of wickedness that can ruin your whole life. It can turn the entire course of your life into a blazing flame of destruction, for it is set on fire by hell itself" (NLT). The AMPLIFIED translation of that verse suggests that the tongue sets "on fire the wheel of birth (the cycle of man's nature)." Your tongue can put a cycle of blessing into motion—or a cycle of cursing.

When Scripture says the tongue is set on fire by hell, one meaning is that the devil tries to get words to come out of your mouth that he can use as an open door to attack your life. The devil well knows you cannot have a negative mouth and a positive life. Scripture says to take up the shield of faith to quench the fiery darts of the enemy (see Ephesians 6:16). Most of those darts

Satan throws at you come into *your* thoughts and out of *your* mouth! That is why sometimes in difficult moments it is best to zip your lips and say nothing. That way you cut off the devil's opportunity to burn you with your own words.

Another faith-hindering habit is letting your thought life run rampant. Negative thoughts give birth to negative words, and both hinder favor. You and I need to control our thoughts, as 2 Corinthians 10:3–5 directs:

> For though we walk in the flesh, we do not war according to the flesh. For the weapons of our warfare are not carnal but mighty in God for pulling down strongholds, casting down arguments and every high thing that exalts itself against the knowledge of God, bringing every thought into captivity to the obedience of Christ.

You need to bring into captivity every argument of the carnal mind, every thought that says, "God didn't do that; it was a coincidence. That wasn't God's protection; that wasn't God's favor on my life." If you will bring your negative thoughts and negative words under control, you will grow in favor and have a positive life.

What Kind of Reporter Are You?

What is the latest breaking news in your life? Your speech is one of the biggest indicators of whether or not you are bringing your thoughts into captivity and having the mind of Christ, as 1 Corinthians 2:16 instructs. It amazes me how many people are negative reporters. They constantly report on all the terrible things taking place in their lives: "My knees hurt; must be early arthritis." "My marriage is on the rocks; we'll be divorced by this time next year." "My kids are in trouble; they are probably on drugs." Have you ever been around someone like that? You begin to wonder if they ever have anything good to say. And they don't—unless and until they are transformed by the renewing of their minds in God's Word.

If you say what you have, you only get what you've got! Take a minute to really let that statement sink in. If you understand it, you will grasp why many people have difficulty growing in favor. You can stunt your growth by reporting on the wrong kind of news, by speaking out what *is* in your life instead of what you can believe God *will do* in your life.

Paul Ruzinsky, senior pastor of our affiliate church in Newaygo, Michigan, gave an excellent example of this one night when he was guest speaker at our midweek service:

> Often when I pray for someone's healing, the sick person is a veritable wealth of information regarding his or her disease. I come across people who know more about the pathology of their diseases than their doctors know. They have spent hundreds of hours researching their illnesses on the Internet, and they rattle off symptoms and treatments as if they were walking medical encyclopedias. But when I ask them, "What does the Word of God say about your illness? What Scripture are you standing on for healing?" they give me a blank look. They cannot come up with a single verse about healing. "I never could memorize Scripture very well," they tell me, or they excuse themselves by claiming, "My memory is not so good anymore."
>
> I don't buy it! They just gave me fifteen definitions of their disease, from memory, out of fifteen different sources they have been studying, and they can name each source. There is *nothing* wrong with their memories—they are just getting their information from the wrong place. They need to study the Word, the source of their healing, more intently than they study their illness. They need to be standing on fifteen different healing verses instead of fifteen medical articles!

Ask yourself what kind of reporter you are. What is the source of your information? Are you giving a good report or an evil report? When God says by His stripes you were healed and you say your sickness is going to be the death of you, then that is an evil report. When God says He left you His peace and you say you are anxious or depressed, then that is an evil report. When God says you can do something and you say you cannot, then that is an evil report. The kind of report you give says a lot about what is down in your heart.

You do not see with your eyes; you see with your heart. And your heart is where your report originates. We talked briefly in chapter 2 about the twelve Israelites Moses sent to spy out the Promised Land. For forty days they canvassed the land. All twelve saw the same thing with their eyes, but they brought back differing reports according to what was in their hearts. Caleb and Joshua saw that the land was good and assured the Israelites they were well able to take it. Caleb reported from his heart: "I brought back word to him [Moses] as it was in my heart" (Joshua 14:7). The other ten, although they agreed the land was a prize, maintained the Israelites could never take it—and God called their report evil (see Numbers 14:36–37). Their report differed from God's spoken word that the land was theirs.

Whose report do you believe in your heart? Whose report do you repeat?

In the gospels, the woman with the issue of blood suffered from her illness twelve long years and "spent all her livelihood on physicians and could not be healed by any" (Luke 8:43). Imagine: Her money was gone, and every doctor said she was a hopeless case. But those were not the sources she chose to believe. And those were not the reports she gave herself or others. She did not say, "It's over. I'm broke. The doctors were no help. I wonder what I did for God to punish me like this. I'm an outcast and I'm getting sicker—I'm probably going to die of this." Not at all. Her heart took her in the opposite direction. She had heard about Jesus, and she chose to take that report as her source instead.

Faith came to her by hearing. She "kept saying to herself, If I only touch His garment, I shall be restored to health" (Matthew 9:21, AMPLIFIED). She refused to be hindered by the doctors' reports or by her financial state, by the crowds that made Jesus difficult to reach or by the unclean status of her condition. She simply *kept on saying* to herself, *I will be well*. She told herself the best days of her life were ahead of her, not behind her. And so it was. God created the fruit of her lips, and she was healed.

Like the woman with the issue of blood, sometimes you have to hear it from *yourself*. Talk to yourself and *keep on saying it*. David did it in Psalm 42:5: "Why are you downcast, O my soul? Why so disturbed within me? Put your hope in God, for I will yet praise him" (NIV). David told himself, "Cheer up—God is on your side. He is yet going to bless, and you will praise Him!" David chose to have faith in God and report from the right Source.

Ruth did the same thing. She did not bemoan the fact that she was a poverty-stricken widow and a foreigner, nor did she expect to starve. She had chosen to dwell among God's people, and the report of her mouth showed her faith in Him. She went out in the morning telling herself and Naomi that she would "glean heads of grain after him in whose sight I may find favor" (Ruth 2:2). She came home loaded down by Boaz with as much grain as she could carry.

Although a number of my examples have been about health, the same principles apply to unleashing the force of favor. What you say is important, but what you believe in your heart is even more important because that is where your words originate. Are you filling your heart with God's Word or the world's reports? The apostle Paul urged Timothy,

> Study and be eager and do your utmost to present your-self to God approved (tested by trial), a workman who has no cause to be ashamed, correctly analyzing and accurately dividing [rightly handling and skillfully teach-ing] the Word of Truth.
>
> 2 Timothy 2:15, AMPLIFIED

Maintain your spiritual health and strength by read-ing, studying and meditating on the Word daily. John 14:26 says that the Helper, the Holy Spirit, will remind you of the things Jesus said. That implies that you are wise to have the Scripture in your heart in the first place so that the Helper *can* jog your memory of it.

Like my everyday run for physical exercise, getting spiri-tual "exercise" daily in the Word is far healthier for you than trying to build your faith in a crisis by running a three-hundred-verse marathon through the Bible, desperately trying to find the verses you need. Like a three-hundred-mile run, that kind of exercise might put you under just when you need to be on top of things the most.

Too Little Too Late

I always like being on top of things. While I cannot anticipate every situation, I do my best not to go into things unprepared. But regardless of whether I know about a situation ahead of time or it arises unexpectedly, if I am caught off guard spiritually I can blame only myself. After all, I have available to me a whole Bible full of truths to put in my heart ahead of time. Hiding God's Word in your heart is the best preparation I know for whatever comes your way.

If I am ever tempted to slack off, I think of a certain fishing boat captain I once knew. I took two of my sons, who were thirteen and nine, out on his boat. We boarded at Ludington, and he took us out to the Pointe to fish for steelhead. After several hours of fun, we headed back to shore at about thirty miles an hour. Samuel, Daniel and I were enjoying the ride when all of a sudden the boat's motor started to sputter. The captain thought he should stop and check it. He lifted up the motor cover, and water began to spew out everywhere. He quickly dropped the cover and tried to restart the motor, but it would not cooperate.

We did not know this at the time, but as we had traveled across the water we had hit a log. That log put a hole bigger than a basketball in the bottom of the boat! It took about sixty seconds from the first sputter of the motor for us to be standing in water.

Grabbing his radio, the captain started shouting, *"Coast Guard! Coast Guard! Mayday! Mayday!"*

The Coast Guard answered right away, "What's the problem, sir?"

The captain yelled, *"We're sinking!"*

"Where are you, sir?" the Coast Guard dispatcher's voice came back.

The captain gave the LORAN-C numbers, so the Coast Guard knew within a quarter of a nautical mile exactly where we were. "We'll be there in twenty minutes," the voice determined.

That response did nothing for our captain. "We're still *twenty minutes* out from shore!" he gasped.

By now the water was around our knees. "Do you have any life jackets?" I asked. He handed me a couple, and I put them on Samuel and Daniel. Then I threw the boys overboard. I pointed them toward shore and motioned, "Head that way!"

I figured with the Coast Guard on its way and a life jacket to hold them up, the boys would be safer in the water than in a sinking boat. I did not want my boys to go down with the ship. I had seen too many movies where a boat sinks and this big old whirlpool sucks everything down.

The water had risen well above my knees, and when I looked at the captain, I saw terror in his eyes. He looked at me and cried out, "I can't swim!"

This is no time for swimming lessons! I thought. *In two or three minutes this boat will sink!*

Spiritually, many Christians do the same thing as our captain. They wait until the doctor says, "It's cancer," or the bank manager says, "We're foreclosing on you," or the spouse says, "I'm leaving," and then they want to learn to swim. They scramble for their Bibles and ask, "Where *is* the verse that covers this—I know it's in here *somewhere*." In the moment of crisis they look for a quick fix to build up their faith and rescue them, but spiritually such a rescue does not always happen. The Word should have been in their hearts already.

When your spiritual boat is sinking and you have only a minute or two before it goes underwater, trying to swim through the Bible to find an applicable verse is doing too little too late. You put yourself in danger by not preparing ahead of time. You cannot wait until panic has grabbed your heart. You have to learn to swim before you get in the boat. You have to put God's Word in your heart *before* a crisis comes, while you have time to study it and comprehend God's will. Put the Word in your heart every day, and the Word will come out in times of trouble. Even under pressure, you will speak in agreement with God out of the abundance of your heart.

Too often we let society and our circumstances tell us what to believe and how to respond. If, for example, you fill yourself with afternoon soap operas and nighttime docudramas, then that is the mind-set you will manifest when you are stressed. But *General Hospital* cannot heal you. A docudrama on how someone fought off his or her swindling ex-spouse will not cure your financial woes. Your doctor's report is not the final report. Again, whose report will you believe?

Proverbs 6:2 says, "You are snared by the words of your mouth." When sickness strikes, you need to declare 1 Peter 2:24: "By his wounds I have been healed." When you face financial difficulty, you need to proclaim Philippians 4:19: "My God shall supply all my needs according to His riches in glory by Christ Jesus." You are not denying that sickness or financial pressure is real; you are professing that a higher law supersedes the laws of the physical realm. Speak the Word over your situation, and the law of divine truth will cause that which is already real in the spiritual realm to manifest in your life.

It is the same with favor. When you need favor the most, you need to declare Jesus' words to you: "I have come that they may have life, and that they may have it more abundantly" (John 10:10). No matter how much favor surrounds you, your negative words can keep it from flowing into your life. Think of it this way: You can do everything we have talked about to "hit the favor switch" and grow in favor. You can position yourself right under the spout where God's favor comes out, so to speak. But opening your mouth to speak negative words is like opening a huge umbrella right over your head. Favor is raining down like a shower all around you, but you are staying high and dry, missing out on what you need the most.

When you need favor the most, you need to already know in your heart that God wants you to be blessed when you go in and blessed when you go out, to be the head and not the tail, to be above your circumstances and not under them. That kind of mind-set planted deep in your heart comes from being in the Word every single day.

By the way, thankfully we did not get sucked under the day our fishing boat went down, and our captain was not forced to "sink or swim." Another boat spotted us and fished us safely out of the water. And although we were rescued in time, I still think learning to swim *before* you get in the boat is a good idea.

A Two-Tongued Sword

God calls things you cannot see in the natural as though they already exist. Look at what the book of Romans says about God's promise to Abraham:

> Therefore, the promise comes by faith, so that it may be by grace and may be guaranteed to all Abraham's offspring—not only to those who are of the law but also to those who are of the faith of Abraham. He is the father of us all. As it is written: "I have made you a father of many nations." He is our father in the sight of God, in whom he believed—the God who gives life to the dead *and calls things that are not as though they were*.
>
> Romans 4:16–17, NIV (italics added)

As a child of God, you are counted among Abraham's offspring. The promise that comes by faith is *for you*. God calls things that are not in your life as though they were, and He wants you to do the same. When you feel weak, God calls you strong. He commands you to say it, too: "Let the weak say, 'I am strong'" (Joel 3:10). When you feel anxious or depressed, say, "Jesus told me, 'My peace I leave with you.'" When you are trying to gain control of your eating habits and lose weight, say, "My body desires healthy food, not comfort food. I have self-control and a metabolism that burns fat. My body works the way God created it to work." When you and your boss or you and your spouse are at odds, say, "I have favor with my boss; we work great together. God uses my boss to bless me." Or say, "My spouse and I love each other; we are going to have a long, awesome life together full of forgiveness and adventure."

Before he even made a move, David declared the great things God would help him accomplish. And he kept on saying them. Before he went out to fight Goliath, he first told King Saul, "Your servant has killed both lion and bear; and this uncircumcised Philistine will be like one of them. . . . The LORD, who delivered me from the paw of the lion and from the paw of the bear, He will deliver me from the hand of this Philistine" (1 Samuel 17:36–37). And David's confession did not stop there. Goliath himself heard it next from David:

> "This day the LORD will deliver you into my hand, and I will strike you and take your head from you. And this day I will give the carcasses of the camp of the Philistines to the birds of the air and the wild beasts of the earth, that all the earth may know that there is a God in Israel."
>
> 1 Samuel 17:46

And so it happened, just as David had spoken.

Think about it—anybody can shout when the giant is lying down. Any army can shout when the walls of the city have crumbled at their feet. But to shout victory *before* it happens is a whole different matter. It calls for faith in the favor of God.

By faith, call those things that are divine truth in the spiritual realm into being in the natural realm. It is not a magic formula or wishful thinking. It is operating within the laws of God's Word. Remember: Proverbs 18:21 says death and life are in the power of your tongue. You can bring death or life into every situation you face. Do not use your words to confirm or mold negative situations in your life. Use your words and God's Word to change those situations. Jesus confirmed the power of the spoken word in John 6:63: "Every word I've spoken to you is a Spirit-word, and so it is life-making" (MESSAGE).

Spirit-words—God's words coming out of your mouth because they are in your heart—are life-making. Revelation 1:16 says when Jesus returns, a two-edged sword comes out of His mouth. With that sword He defeats His enemies. In Greek, *two-edged sword* can actually be translated "two-tongued sword." You have a two-tongued sword coming out of your mouth, too—God's Word. First of all, God says something. His is the first tongue. Then you speak in agreement with it. Yours is the second tongue. God's Word out of your mouth is filled with the same power it had coming out of His mouth. God's Word never goes out without producing an effect. It is never powerless (see Isaiah 55:11). When you speak His Word, His power is behind it.

Let me insert one caution here. Ecclesiastes 8:8 says, "There is no man ruling over the spirit to restrain the spirit" (YLT). One application of that verse is that you cannot force your will on someone else. You do not have authority over another person's spirit. Suppose you are single and see an attractive young woman sitting near you in church. You think, *What a babe! I'm going to claim her. She's going to marry me in Jesus' name!*

That is not using biblical faith. You cannot manipulate other people with your faith, nor can your confession force them to do something. God has given each of us a free will, and your confession does not take it away from someone else. Trying to manipulate another person into doing what you want is the sin of witchcraft. And witchcraft is life-threatening—to you. Those who practice such things will not inherit the Kingdom of God (see Galatians 5:19–21).

Be a Student of the Word

In the area of favor or in any other area you care to name, nothing is as important as having God's Word inside you. Proverbs 15:28 gives good advice: "The heart of the righteous studies how to answer." Make sure you are studying the right textbook—God's Word—daily.

If you study the Word every day, you will not be caught unprepared, sitting in a sinking boat and wishing you had learned to swim. You will not need to attempt a three-hundred-mile Scripture marathon where you hurriedly search everywhere for an applicable verse. You will not try to apply some spiritual "magic formula" where you quickly do one, two and three and hope that—*poof*—you are out of trouble. If you will apply yourself to the Word daily, then when you need something—God's favor to surround you, or healing from an illness, or an angel to shut the lions' mouths as Daniel needed in his day of adversity—you will know that God already has provided all you need.

"Faith is the substance of things hoped for, the evidence of things not seen" (Hebrews 11:1). Confess with your mouth the Word you already have in your heart. Do not report only what you have and get only what you've got. And do not fall for the devil's lie that it is too late for you. If you are alive and still talking, it is not too late! Use your voice to cry out and prepare the way of the Lord in your life. Confess with your mouth what God says is yours, and watch Him release the full force of His favor toward you as you walk out—and speak out—His Word.

6

Straying the Course of Favor

Naomi's Path

House of Bread. That is the literal Hebrew translation of the name *Bethlehem*, the city in which Jesus was born. How fitting a name for the place of His birth, since He called Himself the Bread of Life and told us that anyone who eats of this Bread would live forever. Some eleven hundred years before Jesus was born, however, another family made their home in the city called House of Bread, the family of Elimelech and Naomi. The book of Ruth relates their story.

The genealogy in Ruth chapter 4 begins several generations before Ruth and ends at King David. It shows that Ruth was David's great-grandmother and, according to Ruth 1:1, she and her family lived in the time of the judges. It was not a golden era in Israel's history—many of the judges were dysfunctional, and "everyone did what was right in his own eyes" (Judges 17:6). Mighty men such as Samson and Jephthah led the people, although their own lives were a terrible mess.

God can still use and bless people who have made a mess of things, as we shall soon see. And that is good news for most of us! Even if we stray from the course of His favor, it is never too late to get back on its path.

Ruth's mother-in-law, Naomi, strayed far from the course of favor for a time, yet God used her family line to bring forth the Savior of the world. In Naomi's time, a famine struck the land. She and her husband, Elimelech, relocated from Bethlehem to the land of Moab with their two sons, Mahlon and Chilion. They had been living in the "House of Bread," but because things were tough where God had them, they began to stray off course. They moved to Moab, of all places, about fifty miles away. There the grass somehow looked greener. I am not sure how it could have—Moab was a thoroughly heathen land. The Moabites were the descendants of Lot, arising from his incestuous relationship with one of his daughters, and they worshiped pagan gods.

Many of us stray from the course of God's favor the same way Naomi did. When things get tough, people dive into the pit of despair and often abandon where they are for someplace even worse. In 1933, for example, the president of Studebaker despaired when hard times hit the corporation and it went into receivership. He thought, *It's over!* He committed suicide, not realizing the company's best days were still ahead.

Life has its ups and downs, and in the down times we need to persevere and believe God for favor, not wallow in despair. We will not always be traveling through such valleys in life—just as we will not always have mountaintop experiences. Naomi paid a high price for the course she and her family chose to take in low times. We will come back to that thought, but let's start by looking more closely at this family and the significance of their names.

Prophetic Names Tell the Story

While this was an actual family living out real historical events, I find it fascinating that each member's name had prophetic implications, just as Bethlehem meant "House of Bread." The following list may look daunting, but stay with me—this gets interesting!

The father of the family was *Elimelech*, a name meaning "our God is King." His wife's name, *Naomi*, means "the favor of God." Naomi is particularly interesting for two reasons: First, she carried in her name the focus of this book, the favor of God. Second, at one low point she separated herself from that meaning and took a new name. Arriving back in Bethlehem from Moab, she asked to be called *Mara*, meaning "bitter."

The sons' names, Mahlon and Chilion, are also significant. Both names can be derived from root words having positive or negative connotations. In the negative, *Mahlon* can originate from a root meaning "sickness" or "disease"—which certainly applies to this family's saga since Mahlon died in Moab. For our purposes, though, we will concentrate on the positive root word found in *Mahlon*, which carries the meaning "joyful song." The second son's name, *Chilion*, originates the same way. Its negative connotations are "decimation" or "destruction," also applicable to the story since he died in Moab as well. But again, we will focus on the positive roots, which mean "perfection" or "uprightness."

As for the Moabite daughters-in-law whom the sons married, one was named *Orpah*, from a word meaning "back of the head." The other was *Ruth*, meaning "comeliness" or "beauty." Later in the story Ruth marries *Boaz*, whose name means "redeemer" and who is a type of Christ.

If you are already familiar with the book of Ruth, no doubt you are beginning to see the parallels between their names and the way their story unfolds. Their prophetic names tell the story. To begin with, "God is King" married "the favor of God." When God is King in your life, the favor of God goes with you! Then the couple gave birth to "joyful song" and "perfection" or "uprightness." When God is King and His favor goes with you, it puts a song in your heart and you walk uprightly. When God looks at you, He sees the perfect righteousness of Christ. Before long a test came upon the family. Bethlehem suffered under a lack of bread, so the family looked toward the fertile fields of Moab and left the House of Bread to go where they did not belong—a land where God was *not* King.

Beware such course changes in your own life. You will always have opportunities to return to a place in your life where God was not King, a point before you experienced salvation and His abundant favor. God got Israel out of Egypt all right, but He had a much harder time getting Egypt out of Israel. The Israelites kept whining, "Let's go back to Egypt where we ate leeks and onions" (see Numbers 11:4–6). They had manna from heaven right where they were, but things got a little tough and they craved past pleasures. How quickly they forgot the pain of slavery in Egypt!

Have you ever forgotten the pain of your slavery to sin? The devil will always try to paint a rosy picture of your life B.C.—before Christ. He brings to your mind a picture of yourself at a party. You see yourself laughing and feeling fine, but the devil neglects to bring up the morning after. He does not remind you how hung over you were, leaning over the commode, full of embarrassment, aching in head and heart.

Do not let the enemy fool you into forgetting how hopeless your past was before Christ. The enemy has a course he would like you to walk, going places you should not go and doing things you should not do. But do not walk out from under God's protection. It does not pay to abandon your place in God to go back to your old ways. When you step out of God's will, favor and protection do not follow you. That is why the most miserable people on the face of the earth are not the sinners, but the backsliders. Born-again Christians are new creatures in Christ, and their new nature on the inside is grieved by sin. Of course, sin may indeed be pleasurable for a season. As Proverbs 23:35 says, after a binge the drunkard asks himself, "When shall I awake, that I may seek another drink?" Hebrews 11:25 speaks of "the passing [or temporary] pleasures of sin." But when believers compromise with sin, they leave the place of favor. Their joy, peace and fellowship with God all are affected, and their spirits are in utter misery.

When you are saved and you backslide, you lose your focus on God as King. Your body and mind may try to enjoy that path, but inside, you will be utterly miserable because you also lose your joyful song and your upright lifestyle. God's Spirit keeps witnessing with your spirit, convicting you and calling you back to Himself and the place of His favor.

That was how it was with Naomi. She was utterly miserable in Moab, where her husband, Elimelech (or "God is King"), died. Both her sons—Mahlon, or "joyful song," and Chilion, or "upright lifestyle"—died there as well. Left alone save for her daughters-in-law in a pagan land where God was *not* King, she missed her joyful song and her upright lifestyle. She recognized her need to return to God's land, so when she heard the Lord had visited His people Israel with bread, she determined to go back to Bethlehem.

Once she made her decision, Naomi entreated her daughters-in-law to return to their mothers' houses in Moab, that they might find new husbands and secure a better life than she expected to live as a widow in Bethlehem. Remember how Orpah's name came from the word for "back of the head"? Though she had tears in her eyes, Orpah kissed Naomi good-bye, turned her back on "favor" and walked away.

Ruth, however, took a different course. She showed that her "comeliness" and "beauty," the meanings of her name, were more than skin-deep—she had a depth of character that made her beautiful. Her response to Naomi's entreaty stands among the best known of all Scriptures: "Wherever you go, I will go; and wherever you lodge, I will lodge; your people shall be my people, and your God, my God" (Ruth 1:16). The Bible says Ruth clung to Naomi. In essence, Ruth said, "I'm going to stay with favor [Naomi]. I'm not going to let favor depart from me!"

In the next chapter, we will delve more deeply into how Ruth stayed the course of favor by choosing to follow Naomi. But notice here what Naomi did next:

> Now the two of them went until they came to Bethlehem. And it happened, when they had come to Bethlehem, that all the city was excited because of them; and the women said, "Is this Naomi?"
>
> But she said to them, "Do not call me Naomi; call me Mara, for the Almighty has dealt very bitterly with me. I went out full, and the Lord has brought me home again empty. Why do you call me Naomi, since the Lord has testified against me, and the Almighty has afflicted me?"
>
> Ruth 1:19–21

"Don't call me 'the favor of God,'" she told the women in no uncertain terms. "Call me 'bitter' instead." Blaming

God, she felt God had cursed and afflicted her, but the truth is this: She and her husband chose to walk away from the House of Bread into a cursed place rife with idol worship and other abominable practices. Proverbs 19:3 says, "The foolishness of man ruins his way, and his heart rages against the LORD" (NASB). Put bluntly, people ruin their own lives with their unwise choices, and then they blame God. Such was the case with Naomi/Mara.

Favor Flows in the House of Bread

The decisions you and I make determine the course of our lives. The full force of God's favor is at work only when we walk in obedience to God, doing His will in the place He has put us. Naomi and Elimelech walked away from the place of God's blessing, and the results were catastrophic for their family. Then Naomi's heart raged against the Lord.

Many people today likewise blame God for their circumstances. Yet illnesses, bankruptcies, marital problems or whatever else they are experiencing are not God's fault at all. Those things result from their own unwise choices.

God is not your problem—God is the answer to your problem! The devil is the one who would steal from you, kill things in your life and destroy you, but Jesus came for just the opposite reason, so that you may have life and "have it more abundantly" (John 10:10). "'For I know the plans I have for you,' says the LORD. 'They are plans for good and not for disaster, to give you a future and a hope'" (Jeremiah 29:11, NLT).

God had a good plan in mind for Naomi/Mara, too. She had made a terrible mess of things, but then she returned to the land where God was King. Once Naomi was back where she belonged, favor flowed for her in the House of Bread. Even though she did not immediately recognize it (she was still saying, "God has done this to me"), God's favor was starting to bring her into a place of great blessing. It also flowed mightily toward the daughter-in-law who traveled with her. Ruth was greatly blessed for staying the course of favor, and we will follow her path in the next chapter.

No matter where you have been in the past or where you are now, when you come back where God wants you, His favor starts flowing into your life again. You will find protection, provision and peace in the place where God is King.

7

Staying the Course of Favor

Ruth's Path

The book of Ruth is one of only two Bible books named after a woman. The other is the book of Esther. Ruth was a Gentile woman who came to Israel and married a Jewish prince. Esther was a Jewish woman who lived in a Gentile nation and married a Gentile king. I think we should talk about Ruth and Esther as much as we talk about the great men of the Old Testament such as Abraham, David and Solomon. Both these women's books are full of astounding scriptural lessons and phenomenal stories that illustrate how God moves mightily in people's lives.

In the last chapter we followed the path of Ruth's mother-in-law, Naomi, as she strayed far from the course of God's favor and then eventually returned to it. In this chapter we will follow Ruth's path and glean some amazing lessons from it. Because Ruth stayed the course of favor and refused to be parted from it, God was able to take her from one level of favor to another until she was experiencing so much favor that she could hardly contain it.

Earlier I compared favor to electricity. We all know electric current flows at different voltages: 110, 220, 440. Just as there are different levels of electrical force, some more powerful than others, there are also different levels of favor to experience. We can think of favor in terms of stature, too. Luke 2:52 says, "Jesus grew in wisdom and stature, and in favor with God and men" (NIV). There are different degrees of stature or height—you might be 4-foot-11 or 5-foot-8 or 6-foot-2—and similarly, there are different degrees of favor. The degree or level of favor you experienced a year ago is not where you should still be today. And today's level of favor is not where you should still be a year from now. You should rise to greater heights of favor all the time, as Jesus did.

Ruth continually grew in favor. Her attitude and actions were the key to her extraordinary growth rate. Ruth started with salvation, where favor begins, but she did not stop there. By observing her behavior, we can discover specific things she did to facilitate her rise to new levels of favor. If we will follow in her footsteps, then we, too, can keep growing in the favor of God and men until we cannot contain it all!

Level One: Experiencing Salvation

Jesus Himself tied salvation and favor together when He made His declaration that this is the time when salvation and the free favors of God profusely abound (see Luke 4:19, AMPLIFIED). Salvation is where favor begins (though it need not stop there!). Nothing ever surpasses becoming a child of God and knowing His mercy and grace. Nothing else compares. But as you will discover in your rise to greater levels of favor, God is a generous Father who heaps extra blessings on top of His first gift of salvation.

Ruth made a choice to start with salvation, as must we all. She first married into an Israelite family who worshiped the Lord, though her Moabite family of origin likely worshiped idols. When her husband (Naomi's son) died, rather than returning to her ungodly heritage, Ruth chose to continue walking out her salvation. She accompanied Naomi back to Bethlehem, saying, "Your people shall be my people, *and your God, my God*" (Ruth 1:16, italics added). No more pagan land for her—she came out from among them and made God her King.

Ruth could have turned back to her old ways as Orpah did. And she could have turned bitter like Naomi. Certainly she had intense provocation. Like Orpah and Naomi, Ruth had lost her husband. After that terrible blow, she also faced the loss of her home upon Naomi's departure. Think of it—Ruth faced the certain loss of family no matter which path she chose—she must either part from her beloved mother-in-law or say good-bye to her birth family in Moab. Furthermore, widows in those times held out little hope for a bright future. And as if that were not enough, in Bethlehem Ruth would be a foreigner in a strange land. She knew that as a Moabitess she might very well be reviled and scorned.

It seems Ruth had more reason than most to fall into despair, blame God and turn away, but she adamantly refused to stray from her chosen course. She was so convinced that a better life awaited her along the path of staying with favor that she staked her life on it: "I will die where you die and will be buried there," she told Naomi. "May the LORD punish me severely if I allow anything but death to separate us!" (Ruth 1:17, NLT).

In today's terms, we call that selling out for God. Ruth gave Him her all, and He gave her His best in return, as He always does. If you have not given God your all as Ruth did, that is the first choice you must make to see His favor unleashed. The steps are the same as those for growing in favor: expect, believe and confess. Expect that God wants you to be His child. Second Peter 3:9 makes that very clear: The Lord is "longsuffering toward us, *not willing that any should perish* but that all should come to repentance" (italics added). Then believe and confess: "If you confess with your mouth the Lord Jesus and believe in your heart that God has raised Him from the dead, you will be saved. For with the heart one believes unto righteousness, and with the mouth confession is made unto salvation" (Romans 10:9–10). If you are ready to step into this starting place of favor but are still not sure how, refer to the appendix at the end of this book, which will help you.

Level Two: Steps Ordered by the Lord

One important lesson we can glean from the book of Ruth is that the Lord is the one directing our steps. As we walk with the Lord, His favor brings us into the right places to make the right connections so that He can bring His blessings into our lives. Things do not happen to us by chance or happenstance. God continually orders our steps as His favor surrounds us on every side.

Often the Lord is ordering our steps when we do not even realize it. We might think to ourselves, *Wasn't it great that I happened to be in the right place at the right time? Wasn't it amazing that I ran across that person just then?* Some would call such events coincidence, but they actually result from God moving on our behalf. Psalm 37:23 confirms this: "The steps of a good man are ordered by the LORD, and He delights in his way." God delights in leading us and guiding us, and bringing us into a place of blessing, connections and provision.

It appeared that Ruth and Naomi *just happened* to reach Bethlehem right before the barley harvest. It appeared that Ruth *just happened* to glean in the fields of one of their kinsmen, Boaz, who treated her kindly. In reality, however, there was no "just happened" about it. God was orchestrating Ruth's steps and bringing her into a whole new level of favor.

I like the attitude Ruth displayed the first time she went out to glean the fields: "Ruth the Moabitess said to Naomi, 'Please let me go to the field, and glean heads of grain after him in whose sight I may find favor'" (Ruth 2:2). As a widow, Ruth was so low on the social ladder and so poverty-stricken that she had to glean to keep Naomi and herself alive. Yet *despite* her circumstances, she confessed favor before she walked out the door. What an example for us to follow! We need to confess favor in every circumstance—even the difficult ones.

Gleaning was a kind of social entitlement program Moses had initiated under God's direction. The Lord instructed,

> When you reap the harvest of your land, you shall not wholly reap the corners of your field, nor shall you gather the gleanings of your harvest. And you shall not glean your vineyard, nor shall you gather every grape of your vineyard; you shall leave them for the poor and the stranger: I am the LORD your God.
>
> Leviticus 19:9–10

When a farmer harvested his field or a vineyard owner his vineyard, he was not to pass over it more than once, and he was to leave the corners. What remained was for the poor. The poor still needed to work to gather it—in

God's economy, "if anyone will not work, neither shall he eat" (2 Thessalonians 3:10). Working is important because it builds self-esteem. People who work for their provision see the reward for their efforts, which gives them a sense of value and purpose. God intended for the poor to have some means available to provide for themselves, so He commanded the landowners to leave produce for them to gather.

Among these poor gatherers for the first time, Ruth gleaned behind the reapers. The Bible says, "She happened to come to the part of the field belonging to Boaz, who was of the family of Elimelech" (Ruth 2:3). Again, there was no happenstance about it. Ruth may not have had a clue; she may have simply felt relief at gathering grain enough for an evening's meal. God's plan, though, was for Ruth to marry Boaz, who would redeem her from her difficult situation, as the meaning of his name suggests. Boaz and Ruth would eventually become King David's great-grandparents and the ancestors of Jesus.

God prepared Ruth's path ahead of time, as He does for all His children. Consider the AMPLIFIED translation of Ephesians 2:10:

> For we are God's [own] handiwork (His workmanship), recreated in Christ Jesus, [born anew] that we may do those good works which God predestined (planned beforehand) for us [taking paths which He prepared ahead of time], that we should walk in them [living the good life which He prearranged and made ready for us to live].

Don't ever ask yourself, *Wasn't that occurrence lucky for me?* No! It was God releasing His favor on you by directing your steps. He has already preplanned good works for you and prearranged a good life. Your path, like Ruth's, has been in His mind from the beginning, and if you are following Him, His favor will follow you and He will order your steps.

An Itinerary of Ordered Steps

I remember powerfully experiencing this "ordered steps" kind of favor on a trip to Russia in the late 1980s. Russia was just beginning to open up and I knew God was going to move, so I felt an intense urgency to get over there. I rounded up a couple guys and we boarded a plane. While the events that took place on our trip looked like happenstance on the outside, it was clear to me that God had prearranged everything down to the last detail. We followed an itinerary of ordered steps.

We flew to Helsinki, Finland, and took a boat across to Estonia. From there we traveled to Riga, the capital of Latvia. We did not know a single person there. We checked into a hotel downtown, settled into our room and looked at each other. "Now what?" I asked.

We decided to take a walk and see what the city looked like. We had not been out on the street more than two or three minutes when a man approached and said, "Are you Americans?" When we answered yes, he replied, "My boss wants to buy you dinner."

That sounded good to us since we had no other plans, so we ate dinner with this man's boss. He was probably 6-foot-7 and weighed four hundred pounds, and he was the most flamboyant person I have ever met in my life. He absolutely loved to eat—in fact, when we later brought him to the United States for a visit and took him to Olive Garden, he ate three dinners all by himself!

As we ate dinner with him in Riga, he told us, "My father was a pastor, and he spent twenty years in a prison camp in Siberia. I am a businessman, but I have also started a little church. Tomorrow, I will send my car to pick you up. I want you to visit my city."

He lived about thirty miles away in Jelgava, a military town housing nuclear weapons. Jelgava was closed to outsiders. We were told that no foreigners had been allowed to visit the town since the end of World War II. On the way there, I kept praying, *O Lord, protect us from getting arrested. Lord, have mercy on Jeanie—what would she do without me?*

He took us to a restaurant in Jelgava, where his flamboyant personality again asserted itself. Military officers were all over the place, and he was drawing attention to us by shouting, "Waiter, come here! Bring these men more food!"

Throughout our meal, I prayed with increasing fervency, *Lord, protect us! Help us not to be arrested!*

"You know what?" our host said next. "You should preach here. People in this city need the Gospel."

"That's right," I agreed, "they do."

I figured it was a great but impossible idea—we were not even supposed to be there, much less preach. But after our host paid the bill, within twenty minutes he had rented the town's civic auditorium, the Hall of Culture. Then he went to the newspaper office and paid for an ad that read, "Come hear two world-famous evangelists from America preach about God on Thursday night!"

I do not remember eating anything on Thursday. No, I was not fasting. First, I was not used to being called a world-famous evangelist, and second, I kept thinking to myself, *We could end up in jail!* That thought did nothing for my appetite.

When we arrived at the auditorium Thursday night, it was packed. Not one seat was empty; people stood along every wall. I gave a simple Gospel message explaining God's love and His plan for their salvation. When I finished, I asked those who wanted to receive salvation to raise their hands. Every single person in the building responded! I thought maybe between the interpreter and me, we had been unclear and the people had misunderstood, so I explained the invitation *again* just to be sure. Again, every single hand went up for salvation. They all understood and wanted to get right with God. Communism had left a void or vacuum in the people's hearts, and I will remember the spiritual hunger on their faces as long as I live.

As we spoke later, I told our host, "I believe in the next few years Russia will see a great revival. There is such a hunger here to know God. It would be phenomenal to open a Bible school." Again I thought it was a great but impossible idea. I knew there had not been a Bible school in Russia since the Communist Revolution, and none in the Baltics since WWII when it had come under Communist rule.

"We could do that," our host said.

"What do you mean?" I asked. "There hasn't been a seminary or Bible school in Russia for more than fifty years!"

"We can do it right here," he said. "I can get you a building."

In less than a year we opened a Bible school. Hundreds of students have attended since then, and not long ago while in Florida, Jeanie and I met one. We were told, "He has started a thousand churches and preaching centers since he was graduated." I asked around, and sure enough it was all true. "He's amazing," I was told. "He did everything you heard about."

That is just *one* student. Multiply him by hundreds, and you can scarcely imagine the effect they are having on that country! When did it all start? When we walked outside that Riga hotel and a man came up and said, "My boss wants to buy you dinner." It seemed like coincidence, but it was not happenstance. God orchestrated it. We did not even realize what was going on—in fact, I wondered if we would be the next ones in a prison camp. But because God was ordering our steps, there is no doubt in my mind that millions of people in Russia are saved today.

Level Three: "Handfuls on Purpose"

As the favor of God increases in your life, God's blessing becomes very obvious to you and those around you. Ruth enjoyed this kind of favor when Boaz noticed her among the gleaners and took an interest in her. Once he found out a little about her, he commanded his servants, "Let her glean even among the sheaves, and do not reproach her. Also let grain from the bundles fall purposely for her; leave it that she may glean, and do not rebuke her" (Ruth 2:15–16). He also granted Ruth his protection. A beautiful, unprotected widow among the gleaners might be considered easy prey, so Boaz instructed his young field hands not to touch her.

When you reach this level of favor, people take notice. You become an inspiration to others as they see good things coming your way—you receive raises and promotions, you make the big sales and you stand out in the crowd. But notice something here: While "handfuls on purpose" ultimately come from God, they come *through* men. You enter a whole new realm where you have favor not just with God but with others, too. So far we have talked mainly about God releasing favor toward you, but recall that Jesus grew in favor with both God *and men*. So can you.

How do you reach the place where people desire to bless you with handfuls of favor on purpose? You can take specific actions to increase other people's favor toward you. Ruth purposely did some things that brought a flood of favor from others her way. One thing we already mentioned was that Ruth made choices that kept her on course with favor. Word of her choices got around. When Boaz visited his field and asked about the new gleaner, his workers answered, "It is the young Moabite woman who came back with Naomi from the country of Moab. And she said, 'Please let me glean and gather after the reapers among the sheaves.' So she came and has continued from morning until now" (Ruth 2:6–7).

Notice a few things about the workers' reports. First, they identified Ruth as the Moabitess who chose to come to Bethlehem with her mother-in-law. Second, they identified her as polite—she followed protocol by asking Boaz's overseer for permission to glean in the field. Third, they reported that she was a hard worker who stayed with her task.

Remember I said Ruth's name meant "beauty"? The beautiful qualities inherent in the meaning of her name were immediately apparent to Boaz because Ruth's character showed in everything she did. She could have turned any man's head with her comeliness, but I do not believe she was the sort of young woman who concentrated on turning a man's head. She instead concentrated on the task at hand, providing food for herself and for Naomi. In so doing, she turned Boaz's heart and found favor with him. He urged her to continue gleaning in his field with his young women and not to go elsewhere. He promised her his protection and invited her to refresh herself with the water his servants had already drawn to drink.

Ruth was overcome at this turn of events. The path she chose, though she walked it with favor, was by no means easy! It had taken self-discipline, commitment and sacrifice, probably with little return in the way of kindness from her new hometown. When Boaz treated her kindly, Scripture says she fell on her face, bowed to the ground and asked, "Why have I found favor in your eyes, that you should take notice of me, since I am a foreigner?" (Ruth 2:10).

Why did Ruth find favor? Boaz's reply answered her question:

> "It has been fully reported to me, all that you have done for your mother-in-law since the death of your husband, and how you have left your father and your mother and the land of your birth, and have come to a people whom you did not know before. The LORD repay your work, and a full reward be given you by the LORD God of Israel, under whose wings you have come for refuge."
>
> Ruth 2:11–12

Ruth found favor because her qualities stood out in a crowd. She was faithful, loyal, polite, a hard worker and humble. (It is not customary in our time and place to bow your face to the ground before someone, but in some parts of the world it is still done and is a symbol of humility.) If you want to live a favorless life, live a proud life. But if you want to experience favor, be humble. "Be clothed with humility," 1 Peter 5:5 instructs, "for 'God resists the proud, but gives grace to the humble.'" When you are proud, not only will God resist you, but so will people. When you are humble, grace comes your way (the word for *grace* in that last verse also means "favor"). Understand that humility does not mean crawling on your belly. It means knowing where you came from and realizing that God has made you who you are and put you where you are by His grace on your life. Because Ruth knew that, she chose to follow the God of Israel rather than returning to her foreign gods.

Boaz was highly impressed with Ruth's attitude and actions. The good things she did brought favor her way and made people take notice. Ruth was one favor-chasing woman! She was neither shy nor slack in her pursuit of favor. We need to follow in her footsteps and chase hard after favor.

Ruth was never content to drift off course or stop growing. She knew the salvation of God, He ordered her steps so she was in the right place at the right time, she found favor with Boaz, who sent handfuls on purpose her way, and *still* she pursued more favor. Ruth was not haughty or demanding once she had Boaz's ear. She let him know she was appreciative and thankful. Yet she knew favor opened doors, so she took the opportunity to ask Boaz for even more: "Let me find favor in your sight, my lord," she answered him back, "for you have comforted me, and spoken kindly to your maidservant" (Ruth 2:13).

Ruth's story illustrates that favor can mean the difference between success and failure. Favor opens amazing doors, and it brings blessings our way with which we can turn around and bless others. It even predisposes those in authority to grant our requests, as would happen between Boaz and Ruth. We will cover that more in the next chapter when we talk about even greater levels of favor, but I want to mention one more thing about Ruth here. I believe one reason she experienced such a flood of favor is because not only did she confess favor before she went out, but she also acknowledged the favor with a grateful heart when she came back in! When she returned home to Naomi after one exchange with Boaz, Scripture says Ruth "told her all that the man had done for her" (Ruth 3:16). Ruth spread the word about her redeemer's wonderful works.

The AMPLIFIED translation of Psalm 107:15 urges, "Oh, that men would praise [and confess to] the Lord for His goodness and loving-kindness and His wonderful works to the children of men!" I believe that like Ruth, we will experience a greater flood of favor when we gratefully acknowledge the wonderful works our

Redeemer has already done. Think about what happened in the book of Acts, when the newborn Church grew by leaps and bounds. At Pentecost, visitors from many lands and languages were amazed that they all could understand Jesus' Galilean followers, and notice what they were hearing: "We hear them speaking in our own tongues *the wonderful works of God*" (Acts 2:11, italics added).

The Church grew by three thousand that day, and it continues to add to its numbers whenever believers speak out the wonderful works of God. Psalm 107 also urges, "Let the redeemed of the Lord say so, whom He has delivered from the hand of the adversary" (verse 2, AMPLIFIED). Your Redeemer has done great things for you. Besides granting you salvation, perhaps He has delivered you from alcohol, gambling or another addiction. Perhaps He has restored your broken marriage and family relationships.

Spread the word about your Redeemer's glorious acts! People in your hometown may have the same problems and bondages you had, but they do not want to hear a sermon or study theology. Did you want to hear someone preach at you when you were straying? Probably not. Although a pastor's preaching or a seminary professor's theology has its place, what draws people to God is the word of *your* testimony. When people find out you suffered from the same hang-ups they have and God did something for you that made all the difference, *that* draws them. They want to hear from somebody on their street or in their workplace that God is real. They want to see that He is alive and at work in people's lives today. They want to witness the force of His favor in action in your life. If you will acknowledge aloud the favor God has already shown you, you can make all the difference for someone else and help deliver him or her from the hand of the adversary.

Turn the Key

If you find that you are not experiencing more and more favor in your life the way Ruth did, keep in mind that getting into the path of favor is like getting into your car. Once inside, you are surrounded by your automobile, just as you are surrounded continually with favor. But if you do not put your car key into the ignition and turn it, you are going nowhere.

Just as you need to take action to start your car, you need to take specific steps to grow into greater levels of favor. Like Ruth, you need to choose God as your King. Then walk in faithfulness and humility, letting your good character be self-evident. God will order your steps as you stay at the tasks He puts before you. Follow Ruth's lead in confessing favor both coming and going. Those are some concrete steps you can take to turn the key in the ignition, so to speak, and move into favor. And like Ruth, as you grow in favor you will go to new places in God.

8

Grow in Favor,
Grow in Leadership

Favor can be found at all levels of leadership. You do not need to be on the top rung of the corporate ladder to be a leader. You do not even need to make it to a middle management rung. No matter what your official title in the business world—no matter if you even *have* a title or are one of many workers on the assembly line—by taking steps to grow in favor, you will grow in influence and leadership ability.

Whether you are on the corporate ladder, the social ladder or any other ladder, you can lead from the bottom up if you are walking in favor. As you rise to new levels of favor, you will rise to new levels of influence. You can learn how to "lead up" from a position of favor, asking people in authority for the things you need. In the Old Testament, both Esther and Nehemiah prefaced their requests to their kings with words such as "if I have found favor in your sight," and both saw their requests quickly granted due to the favor they enjoyed (see Esther 7:3 and Nehemiah

2:5). When you have favor, you receive answers you might otherwise be denied without favor working on your behalf. People respond not just to your requests, but to you—the more you learn to use the right approach and attitude, the more you will begin to see your requests granted.

You also can learn to lead in blessing others with your favor. That was one of Jabez's desires in his well-known prayer for favor: "Oh, that You would bless me indeed, and enlarge my territory, that Your hand would be with me, and that You would keep me from evil, that I may not cause pain!" (1 Chronicles 4:10). Jabez desired that his territory—the place where his influence was felt—would be enlarged so he might touch people's lives. He had a heart to bless others and even prayed that he might not cause pain. The meaning of his name was significant, too, like the Old Testament names we discussed earlier. It meant "pain," but Jabez did not want to live up to his name. He asked for the opposite, that he might be a blessing, and God granted him his request.

Like Jabez, do you desire more positive influence in people's lives? Bless others, and the more favor you sow, the more you will reap. The more favor you reap, the more you will have to sow. You will reach a point where you have so much favor being released on you that you cannot even contain it—you have to find some way to spread it around. That is a *good* problem to have! You certainly do not want to keep all your blessings to yourself or you will become like the Dead Sea, a reservoir where everything flows in but nothing flows out. That is a quick way to stagnate and to kill your growth process. Learning to be a channel of God's favor is one of the biggest steps you can take to grow in that favor.

Jesus approached leadership from the opposite direction of most how-to books you find today on being a leader. He told His disciples, "You know that the rulers of the Gentiles lord it over them. . . . Yet it shall not be so among you; but whoever desires to become great among you, let him be your servant." Then He added, "And whoever desires to be first among you, let him be your slave—just as the Son of Man did not come to be served, but to serve" (Matthew 20:25–28).

Leadership does not start with getting people to follow you. Leadership starts with being worthy to be followed. It starts with leading yourself. In Acts 20:28, Paul makes this point to the church's leaders: "Therefore take heed to yourselves and to all the flock." Note the leaders were to take heed to *themselves* first, and then the flock. According to 1 Timothy 3, about a dozen of the qualities for leadership in an elder or deacon have to do with character, while only one or two have to do with ability.

Leadership starts with you—if you cannot lead yourself, you cannot lead anyone else. If you will take heed to yourself first—seeing to it that God is your King, that you stay on the course of favor and that you walk in humility—then you will lead the way, and others will follow and be blessed through you.

Level Four: "Leading Up" with Favor

In the preceding chapter we talked about experiencing salvation, having your steps ordered by the Lord and receiving handfuls of favor on purpose. Among Old Testament personalities, Ruth stood out in demonstrating how to grow into those levels. She also excelled in this next level, "leading up" with favor, but she was not alone. If ever there was anyone who knew how to lead a leader, it was Nehemiah. He was the trusted cupbearer of King Artaxerxes I of Persia.

Nehemiah the cupbearer was a Jew, and the day came when he heard a report that Jerusalem's walls were broken down and the gates burned. This news greatly troubled him, and apparently he could not get it off his mind, even as he handed wine to the king. Persian monarchs believed that just being in their presence should make anyone happy, so appearing depressed in the presence of the king was an affront punishable by death. The king confronted Nehemiah, asking, "Why is your face sad, since you are not sick? This is nothing but sorrow of heart" (Nehemiah 2:2).

Understandably, Nehemiah was horrified that his sorrow showed. "I became dreadfully afraid," he said in Nehemiah 2:2. He knew the king's next words could be "Off with your head!" Immediately he humbled himself and explained, "May the king live forever! Why should my face not be sad, when the city, the place of my fathers' tombs, lies waste, and its gates are burned with fire?" (Nehemiah 2:3).

It was a daring thing to say, but Nehemiah hoped the king would sympathize with him. Thanks to the position of favor Nehemiah held—and to his intense relief—Artaxerxes did understand. "What do you request?" he asked Nehemiah (see verse 4).

Nehemiah's answer is full of wisdom about how to influence a leader:

> So I prayed to the God of heaven. And I said to the king, "If it pleases the king, and if your servant has found favor in your sight, I ask that you send me to Judah, to the city of my fathers' tombs, that I may rebuild it."
>
> Nehemiah 2:4–5

Observe what Nehemiah did first. He was standing on shaky ground with the king, so before he said another word, he prayed.

The number one thing you need to do before you approach your boss or another person in authority is pray. Short prayers such as *Lord, help me!* can be very effective. Sometimes people think, *I've got to have this huge prayer session—I'll go home and pray for an hour.* But you can do more in ten seconds of heartfelt prayer than in an hour later on, after the crisis.

Furthermore, when other people share a need with you and say, "Will you pray for me?" do not send them away with a promise that you will pray later. Sometimes the best thing is to grab their hands right then and pray a ten- or fifteen-second prayer. The same is true when facing a sticky situation under a leader, as Nehemiah did. Take a minute right then to request God's help.

Next Nehemiah made a request, not a demand. Did you ever notice that walking up to the boss and demanding "I've *got* to have" this or that seldom goes over well? Nehemiah's attitude was humble and submissive. He prefaced his request with "If it pleases [you], if [I have] found favor in your sight." Then he requested, "I ask that you send me," and the king was moved to grant his request.

The good character Nehemiah displayed as a trustworthy cupbearer stood him in good stead that day. He stayed connected to his head for one thing, and his right attitude while making his request calmed the king and prompted him to help Nehemiah.

Ask and You Shall Receive

Ruth's excellent character and attitude stood her in good stead, as well, and led to her receiving the favor of both Boaz and the Lord. This allowed her to "lead up" with favor. Boaz was already aware of her good reputation and had shown kindness toward her, so at her mother-in-law's urging Ruth approached Boaz with a daring request.

It was considered a great tragedy in Israel if a woman's husband died without leaving an heir, and the Law made provision for her by laying the responsibility on a close relative to marry her and provide the heir. Prompted by Naomi, Ruth proposed marriage to the wealthy and renowned Boaz, who was indeed a relative.

Knowing the magnitude of the request, Naomi and Ruth took great pains with the preparations. Naomi wanted to see her daughter-in-law, who had been so good to her, secure and happy, so she told Ruth (my paraphrase), "Wash yourself, put on some ointment, get out that Chanel No. 5 perfume, and wear your best dress!"

This was wise, for it is good to make oneself attractive. One should not dress immodestly and seductively, for the idea is to turn the heart, not the head. But that does not mean that a person cannot dress attractively.

Years ago in Bible college, I had a friend whose father, a well-known missionary, was of the same mind as Naomi on this subject. One young woman set her cap for my friend, so she prayed first, then approached his father. Now, she was a nice girl and cute, but she did not make the most of her looks. Her modesty was a precious trait, but her style was drab and unappealing. She usually wore what I call Mother Hubbard dresses.

My friend's father knew and liked the girl, so he told her, "I would like nothing better than to have you become my daughter-in-law, but"—and at this point he pulled out his wallet and handed her three hundred dollars—"go buy yourself some new clothes before you approach my son!"

You may think, *But what about turning the young man's heart, not his head? The Bible says God looks on the heart.* The father viewed it this way: The girl wanted to marry his son, not God. And his son might not get to know her inner beauty if he could not get past her outer lack of style. The girl took the fatherly advice and won the young man's favor, and they were married.

Apparently, Naomi knew Boaz might notice the outside, too. Like my friend's father, she saw to it that the girl in question was looking her best! And she coached Ruth further: "Then it shall be, when he lies down, that you shall notice the place where he lies; and you shall go in, uncover his feet, and lie down; and he will tell you what you should do" (Ruth 3:4).

It was a humbling action, but Ruth made a practice of humility, which is one reason she was so successful. First, she was not too proud to take good advice. "All that you say to me I will do," she answered Naomi (Ruth 3:5). Then, she uncovered Boaz's feet and lay down, both a bold request on her part for his protection and an extremely submissive gesture. To touch and hold someone's feet in that culture was the act of a humble person or servant, as Jesus showed again hundreds of years later washing His disciples' feet. When Ruth had Boaz's attention, she spoke her request: "Take your maidservant under your wing" (Ruth 3:9).

Boaz understood her marriage proposal and knew it was in keeping with the Law. He praised her for her kindness in not going after the younger men, and—this is favor at its best—he said, "And now, my daughter, do not fear. *I will do for you all that you request*, for all the people of my town know that you are a virtuous woman" (Ruth 3:11, italics added). Boaz got up in the morning and immediately followed through with fulfilling Ruth's request. He went to the city gate to settle the matter of the marriage, but even before he did that, he asked Ruth for her shawl so he could heap extra favor on her. He placed six measures of barley in her shawl, probably equivalent to at least eighty or ninety pounds, so she could carry provisions home to Naomi.

In the ancient world a shawl was often used to carry things. In some parts of the world today, shawls are still used as an incredibly easy way to carry a heavy load. When we lived with the Otomi Indians in Mexico, Jeanie used a type of shawl they called an *ayate* to carry our son Joshua when he was small. It made his naptime very convenient—

we would just hang him in a quiet spot in the *ayate*. Ruth could carry quite a load in her shawl, but understand that Boaz heaped on the favor until she had all she could possibly carry. It would not have broken the bank for him to give her more, but she had no way to contain it. As it was, his gift was so generous that he had to help Ruth lift and settle the load so she could manage it (see Ruth 3:15).

When you enjoy this degree of favor, God heaps on you all you can carry. He loads on all the favor you can possibly contain. It is as if He is asking, "How much can you carry? How much do you want? I will do all for you that you request." You receive good measure, pressed down and shaken together until it is running over (see Luke 6:38).

Often that kind of favor comes to you *from* God but *through* other people. If you maintain your trustworthy reputation and approach your leaders with the right attitude, it will increase the likelihood that they will grant your requests. Because they have consistently observed your good character and integrity, they will be motivated to heap on you all the blessings you can carry. It was the way Nehemiah and Ruth experienced this kind of favor, and it can happen for you.

Certainly instances will occur when your immediate request is not granted, but remember that the way you choose to behave at those times can put you in a position of favor for your future requests. As Jesus said, "He who humbles himself will be exalted" (Matthew 23:12).

Why Favor Does Not Flow

The time may come when you think you are doing everything right, but favor simply is not flowing your direction in the workplace. How can you find out why favor does not flow at your place of employment? I recommend checking the following things.

How is your attitude on the job? First, make sure you are "working as unto the Lord." "Whatever you do, work at it with all your heart, as working for the Lord, not for men" (Colossians 3:23, NIV). A Christian employee should stand out as an excellent worker. You not only work for your boss, but you also work for the Lord, so do the best possible job in everything you do. Your performance should never be second-rate. You should never be the employee who shows up a half hour late, takes fifteen minutes extra on break or stands gossiping at the time clock while waiting for the *exact* second to arrive before punching in. That is not how a Christian employee serves his or her employer. You should be known for doing everything with excellence!

Do you carry bitterness and resentment? If you are bitter or resentful against your boss or coworkers, your actions will give you away. "I will complain in the bitterness of my soul," Job said (Job 7:11), and you will do the same if you are bitter. One thing no employer appreciates is an unpleasant, complaining employee. Whether you complain aloud or inwardly, a bad attitude likely has bitterness and resentment at its root and needs to be dealt with before it adversely affects you, your productivity and the favor on your life.

Are you expecting, believing and confessing? We covered these steps toward growing in favor already, but they bear repeating. Are you taking these steps in your place of employment? Make sure you carry into your workplace the spiritual lessons you learn, and expect to grow in favor there, as elsewhere. What are you saying about having favor on the job? Remember that God creates the fruit of your lips.

Are you in the right place? I have heard it said that you need to be in a place where you are celebrated, not tolerated. We all need a place of favor. As an employee who is working as unto the Lord, you should be a blessing to your employer. If your efforts are not appreciated and acknowledged, if no favor is forthcoming and your ideas and requests fall on deaf ears, you may be in the wrong place working for the wrong people.

Boaz urged Ruth to stay in his fields, the place where she found favor. Stay where God's favor flows to you; do not stray into a place where it stops. If you find yourself in such a place, reconsider your position, as Naomi did. Check your own attitudes and actions first, and then move in a new direction until you find a place where you are favored once again.

Level Five: Blessed to Be a Blessing

The Bible tells us, "Give, and it will be given to you: good measure, pressed down, shaken together, and running over will be put into your bosom" (Luke 6:38). When you learn to lead in blessing others and sowing favor into others' lives, you will lead in reaping favor back. The Lord will reward you.

One beautiful thing about Ruth's character was that she did not hoard her blessings for herself. She went from not having enough to having more than enough, and she found ways to bless another by providing for her mother-in-law. As Ruth shared her blessings, they began to multiply back to her. In a few short weeks, she went from being a poor gleaner in the field to being the wife of the field's owner, Boaz.

Boaz could not help but notice how Ruth blessed her mother-in-law, and he blessed Ruth back with his words: "The LORD repay your work, and a full reward be given you by the LORD God of Israel, under whose wings you have come for refuge" (Ruth 2:12). He also blessed her with his actions, inviting her to take her meal with him and his reapers. What Ruth did in response is significant: "She sat beside the reapers, and he passed parched grain to her; and she ate and was satisfied, *and kept some back"* (Ruth 2:14, italics added).

Why would Ruth "keep some back" out of what she was given? I believe she displayed a Kingdom principle—a part of everything you receive is not meant for you. You are supposed to keep some back. The first part is meant for honoring God with a tithe, and a part is to sow into others, and a part is for saving or investing. You need to honor God with a tithe to see His favor on your finances, you need to sow into others to reap a harvest yourself, and you need to save if you want God to bless your "storehouse."

You may think, *We can't do all that—we barely get by as it is!* If that is the case, maybe you are not applying the principle that a portion of everything you receive is meant for you to sow. If you will consistently do the following, then I believe over time you will do far better than to barely get by.

First, make sure you are honoring God with the first tenth of your income. That positions you for God's blessings to flow:

> "Bring all the tithes into the storehouse,
>   That there may be food in My house [the local
>   church],
>   And try Me now in this,"
> Says the LORD of hosts,
> "If I will not open for you the windows of heaven
> And pour out for you such blessing
> That there will not be room enough to receive it."
>
> Malachi 3:10

God's blessing makes all the difference! We live much better on 90 percent of our income with God's blessing on it than we would 100 percent without His blessing.

Next, bless others with a portion of your income. You truly are blessed to be a blessing. You may be tempted to rationalize, *I tithe, and maybe I can even save a little, but money to give others just isn't there right now. When I get more, I'll give more.* Beware of that philosophy. You can deceive yourself into thinking that if you ever strike it rich, then you will be a generous giver, but it does not work that way. Jesus said he who is faithful with little will also be faithful with much (see Matthew 25:23). What you do with a handful is the same as what you will do with a wheelbarrow full or even a warehouse full. More money will not make the difference in your generosity. Remember the widow's mite? She gave only two small coins, yet Jesus said her gift was greater than all the rest. That widow would have been a generous millionaire. Start giving right where you are.

Also, begin today to build a storehouse, which is the portion you save or invest. I find it amazing that 50 percent of Americans do not have a savings account or any type of investment. Deuteronomy 28:8 promises, "The LORD will command the blessing on you in your storehouses and in all to which you set your hand." How can the Lord bless your storehouses if you do not have any? If you have not done so already, you need to start a storehouse. Start with whatever amount you can, even if it is small. God can bless your storehouse only if you have one!

Favor at Its Best

Ruth was not the only one who found increasing favor as she shared her blessings. Boaz, too, reaped a rich reward for sowing into others—far richer than the obvious wealth he already possessed in his crops and fields. The Lord blessed him with a wife who was beautiful both inside and out and with a son, Obed, the father of Jesse, the father of King David. And through that line God sent the King of Kings, Jesus.

Then there was Naomi, with whom our story from the book of Ruth started. When Naomi took a serious look at the path she was walking, she decided to stop straying from the land of favor and go back to the "House of Bread." She had experienced heartache, changed her name to Mara and complained against the Lord—not unlike many of us when we make poor choices, reap trouble and then blame God for the results. But the ending of her story gives hope to us all.

Naomi could have sat in the corner of her hovel for the rest of her days and moaned about her dire circumstances. She could have let Ruth provide for her as best a gleaner could and done nothing for Ruth or anyone else in return. Instead Naomi decided to get up and invest herself in someone else, rather than focusing on her own woes. She sowed favor into Ruth, using her wisdom and experience to help Ruth secure a husband and home. After Naomi did so, look how both God and man released favor back to her:

> Then the women said to Naomi, "Blessed be the LORD, who has not left you this day without a close relative; and may his name be famous in Israel! And may he be to you a restorer of life and a nourisher of your old age; for your daughter-in-law, who loves you, who is better to you than seven sons, has borne him." Then Naomi took the child and laid him on her bosom, and became a nurse to him. Also the neighbor women gave him a name, saying, "There is a son born to Naomi." And they called his name Obed. He is the father of Jesse, the father of David.
>
> Ruth 4:14–17

And from David's line came the Messiah.

The favor you spread around will come back to you in greater and more powerful ways. "Whatever good anyone does, he will receive the same from the Lord," according to Ephesians 6:8. I like the paraphrased version of that: "Whatever you make happen for others, God will make happen for you."

Favor at its best flows both ways—from God and others to you, and from you to other people. Favor at its best surrounds you on all sides—in your family life, as with Naomi, Ruth and Boaz; in your workplace, as with Nehemiah and King Artaxerxes; in your friendships; in your church; everywhere you go.

Favor at its best also enhances your ability to "lead up" in making requests of those in authority over you. No matter what corporate or social position you find yourself in, you will begin to see your requests granted as you grow in favor.

Your own leadership abilities and influence will grow, too, as you grow in favor. When you are enjoying favor at its best, you may find yourself moving into positions and spheres of influence you never thought possible before you began to experience the full force of God's favor. As Ruth followed her destitute mother-in-law back to Bethlehem, she probably did not picture herself becoming the wife of a rich and powerful man, much less an ancestor of the King of Kings. But remember: Her ability to lead others started with her ability to lead herself. If you want to grow in leadership as Ruth did, you must first display good character and integrity in whatever you do. And the more you are blessed, the more you must seek to bless others.

You are truly blessed to be a blessing, and one of the greatest blessings of all is to enjoy favor at its best.

9

Fair Warning about Favor

They say the best things in life are free, but that does not necessarily mean that those things come easy. The best things in God are not easily attained, free though they are.

God gave the Promised Land to Israel, yet the Israelites had to exert great effort to possess it. They fought to dislodge the pagan nations who lived there, to capture the walled cities and to dispossess the giants who stood in their way. It was a land well worth fighting for—Scripture describes how it flowed with milk and honey and how the grape clusters were so enormous that it took two men to carry them on a pole (see Numbers 13). How the Israelites battled to possess that gift from God!

The Israelites' possession of the Promised Land is a type, or picture, for us of living the victorious Christian life. That land of abundant blessings was meant to foreshadow for us what living in the flow of God's favor would be like. But if we want God's best, then we, too, must "fight the good fight of faith," as 1 Timothy 6:12 says. The Christian life has been called a "fight from the womb to the tomb." Sometimes we must fight the world, the flesh and the devil in order to experience all the blessings God has for us. Like the children of Israel, we must exert the effort necessary to possess our "Promised Land."

Once Israel secured the Promised Land, the dangers did not end. The people still faced many battles, both physical and spiritual. Once we experience God's favor and walk in His blessings, the dangers do not end for us, either. With every blessing comes potential danger. Heed this fair warning about favor: It is often accompanied by its own set of difficulties.

Experiencing a greater release of favor in your life does not mean you will no longer face problems or trials. There is no room to be a weak-kneed, milquetoast believer when you are growing in favor. In fact, the more that favor is unleashed, the more you may discover that some new troubles also are headed your way. Such difficulties are a part of life. I have yet to meet anyone who claims Job 5:7 or hangs the verse on their refrigerator, but it is part of Scripture all the same: "Yet man is born to trouble as surely as sparks fly upward" (NIV). Trouble will come, but facing adversity does not mean you are out of favor with God. As Psalm 34:19 says, "A righteous man may have many troubles, but the LORD delivers him from them all" (NIV).

The value of living in the favor of God far outweighs any obstacles that might accompany His favor. And forewarned is forearmed. If you are aware of the dangers that accompany favor, you will be better able to overcome them. When storms are brewing, your belief in God's favor will not be shaken. When not everyone rejoices about watching you rise to the top, you will understand that such reactions are no surprise. When others who seemed to enjoy God's favor come to ruin because of their lifestyles, you will perceive the cause and take heed lest the same thing happen to you.

Let's take a closer look at some of the dangers surrounding favor so they will not catch you off guard.

The Most Obvious Danger of Favor

The most obvious danger that accompanies favor is simply that you will fall from it, as the Bible clearly shows in Hebrews 12:15. We must look diligently "lest any man fail of the grace of God" (KJV) or lest anyone "[forfeit] the grace of God" (NEB). *Grace* in those Bible versions can also be translated as "favor." Another version paints a painful picture of how you can literally be "falling behind from the favour of God" (ROTHERHAM). The rest of the verse in Hebrews 12:15 describes how such a fall happens: ". . . lest any root of bitterness springing up trouble you, and thereby many be defiled" (KJV). If you allow bitterness into your life, it will stop the flow of favor.

People often think that by holding on to bitterness they can get even with the person who wronged them. They think their resentment and unforgiveness somehow pays back their offender—but that is not how bitterness works. As my wife, Jeanie, often says, becoming bitter is like drinking poison and waiting for the other person to die. *You* are the one who pays the price for your unforgiveness. *You* are the one who gets hurt, particularly since bitterness causes you to fall behind the favor of God.

We must be diligent about forgiving. "Whenever you stand praying, if you have anything against anyone, forgive him," Jesus said, "that your Father in heaven may also forgive you" (Mark 11:25). I am certain Jesus expected us to pray every day, so in effect He is telling us here, "Every day, check your heart. Make sure you don't hold something against someone. If you do, don't let it take root. Show that person grace and favor, and My Father will do the same for you."

Being diligent about forgiveness is like being diligent about gardening. Jeanie loves to garden, so we garden. Every week, twice a week or more, I pull weeds. I remember one time, though, when I did not give our garden the diligent attention it needed. I thought I could ignore my weed-pulling task for a couple of weeks, and the day I went back out to check the garden, I was shocked. I had fallen behind—way behind. The weeds that had started as innocent-looking, easy-to-pull sprouts had now taken over. Some towered like trees above our struggling little vegetable plants, and their root systems were massive, sapping up the moisture and nutrients intended for our garden plants and robbing us of a good harvest.

If you let bitterness into your heart, it will do the same, putting down massive roots that grow harder and harder to pull out. Bitterness will defile you and your relationships with others. But bitterness is easily overcome if you do not let it establish roots. That is why Jesus said if you have anything against anyone, take care of it right away. Remove any sign of bitterness daily by forgiving. Fall behind in dealing with bitterness, and you will fall behind in favor. In fact you will "fail to gain God's favor," as the E. J. Goodspeed translation of Hebrews 12:15 warns.

Forgiveness, on the other hand, is an amazing thing. Forgiveness frees you and returns you to a position of favor. Forgiveness allows the favor to flow again.

The "Look at Me!" Syndrome

Another danger that can accompany favor is the "Look at Me!" syndrome. When things go your way and you enjoy blessing and increase, it can be tempting to give yourself credit where credit is not due. The Lord warned the Israelites about this danger in Deuteronomy 8. He had just promised them a host of blessings, saying that He was bringing them into a good land where they would lack nothing. Then He added,

> Beware that you do not forget the LORD your God . . . lest—when you have eaten and are full, and have built beautiful houses and dwell in them; and when your herds and your flocks multiply, and your silver and your gold are multiplied, and all that you have is multiplied; when your heart is lifted up, and you forget the LORD your God . . . then you say in your heart, "My power and the might of my hand have gained me this wealth."
>
> And you shall remember the LORD your God, for it is He who gives you power to get wealth, that He may establish His covenant which He swore to your fathers, as it is this day.
>
> Deuteronomy 8:11–14, 17–18

Your success comes from God and His favor, not from your own ingenuity. When you succeed, resist the temptation to think it is all your own doing. God gives you the ideas, abilities, connections and power to be successful both financially and in other ways. When God pours out His favor on you, you must make sure you do not flaunt it or take credit for yourself.

We followed some of Joseph's story in chapter 3 and saw how growing in favor with God and men kept Joseph continually rising to the top. Joseph knew at an early age that his dreams and visions were from God, yet as a young man he could not resist falling prey to the "Look at Me!" syndrome. He was seventeen at the time, the eleventh of twelve sons and greatly favored by his father. When he dreamed that his parents and brothers would bow before him, he simply lacked the maturity and wisdom to keep it to himself. Not once but twice he approached his family to inform them about his dreams.

You can imagine how well that went over. His father, who already had singled out Joseph by giving him that famous coat of many colors, rebuked him. And his brothers "hated him yet the more for his dreams, and for his words" (Genesis 37:8, KJV). Had Joseph been a little older and wiser, he might have known that sometimes when God promotes you, it is smarter to keep your mouth shut. Joseph set himself up for some serious persecution when he flaunted the favor he enjoyed, which leads us to the next danger—when the favor of God is on your life, not everyone is going to be happy about it.

Envying Others Who Enjoy Favor

Joseph's brothers scorned and ridiculed him, asking in effect, "What's so special about *you?*" Their pride was hurt by the very thought of Joseph ruling over them, but secretly they envied him (see Genesis 37:8–11). The same envy came upon the Philistines when Isaac reaped the blessings God promised to his father, Abraham. In Genesis 22, God told Abraham He would multiply his descendants and prosper them. By Genesis 26:13–14, Scripture says Isaac "continued prospering until he became very prosperous; for he had possessions of flocks and possessions of herds and a great number of servants. So the Philistines envied him." Like Joseph's brothers, the Philistines criticized and attacked the one whom they saw enjoying favor.

When you notice other people enjoying favor, watch out that envy and pride do not make you ask, "Why do *they* get that? Why not *me?* They have it all, and I'm getting nothing." The Bible says, "Rejoice with those who rejoice" (Romans 12:15). You ought to be happy to see others experience favor, but not everyone displays that attitude. Many people have a spirit of poverty that causes them to complain when someone else gets blessed. They think, *There is just one pie, and it's unfair that this person got such a big slice—now there is less for me!*

God has an unlimited supply of pie. His blessings never run out. You never need to worry that there is less for you because someone else is blessed. When you notice favor on someone else, your first response should be, "Yes! Fantastic!" When your coworker is promoted, be the first to congratulate him. When your neighbor pulls in with a new car, share her excitement and say, "I'm happy for you!" Remember: As we discovered in Ruth's story, one key to walking in increasing favor is to give favor to others. Guard against envying others who enjoy favor—be glad and rejoice with them instead.

Deceiving Yourself about Sin

A dangerous deception about sin can sometimes accompany favor. When God's favor rests on people, they sometimes deceive themselves by thinking it signifies God's blanket approval of their entire lifestyle, and that He winks at or overlooks their sinful areas. Yes, there are times when people whose lives are a terrible mess experience favor, but that does not mean He stamps His seal of approval on all their actions. God is merciful and gracious, and His favor is so great that He does not always pull back His blessings when someone is in sin. Rather, He intends His favor to draw people back to Him. Consider the question Romans 2:4 asks: "Or do you despise the riches of His goodness, forbearance, and longsuffering, not knowing that the goodness of God leads you to repentance?"

Recall that God used Naomi to benefit her daughter-in-law Ruth. That did not mean, however, that God approved of all Naomi's unwise decisions. And His favor on their lives did draw Naomi closer to Him.

God also used Samson during the time of the judges. In many areas Samson did not even come close to exemplifying a godly lifestyle. He never overcame his serious sins, perhaps thinking that since God's favor rested on him from time to time to accomplish mighty feats, everything must be okay. God must approve of his lifestyle, since God still blessed and used him. In the end, such self-deception ushered in Samson's downfall.

The time of the judges was one of the saddest in Israel's history. Many of the judges' lives were a mess. Samson was not alone in his self-deceptions, but his case is perhaps the most astonishing. At the age of twenty he defied his parents and demanded they arrange his marriage to a Philistine girl who caught his eye. His parents begged him to reconsider, to marry a girl from their own people, but Samson was already deep in the throes of his lifelong battle with lust—a battle he never won. His Philistine beauty worshiped pagan gods, but all Samson saw was her outer charm. "Get her for me," he urged his father, "for she looks good to me" (Judges 14:3, NASB).

Now, good looks are nice, but they only go skin deep. You need a lot more than "she looks good to me" or "he looks good to me" for a marriage to work. Looks change, so you had better look for beauty on the inside, not just the outside! Samson had too big a problem with his eyes to do that. He married his Philistine—and the marriage lasted a whole ten days.

One time when Samson was on his way to see this girl, a lion attacked. The power of God came on him, and he tore the lion apart with his bare hands. Was he anointed of God? Obviously. Did he harbor sin in his life? Certainly. Another time ten years later, he traveled to the city of Gaza and slept with a prostitute. He got up at midnight, approached the city gates, pulled out the doors and poles and walked up a mountain with them on his back. Was that supernatural power from God? Absolutely. Did it negate the sin in his life and mean that God approved? Absolutely not!

Yet with all his faults, Samson judged Israel for twenty years. You probably know how his story ends. He never conquered his sinful lust, and twenty years later he fell for Delilah. She betrayed him and cut off his hair, and the Philistines captured him and poked his eyes out. (That took care of the lust of his eyes the hard way!) He pushed a millstone around and around in the Philistine prison, and the Philistines made sport of him until his death.

All the while that God's favor visited him, Samson deceived himself into thinking he did not need to clean up his act. He never overcame his sin, and it ruled his life until his death. How many of us are like him? If you are ever tempted to think, *I worship God, I feel His presence, I pray and He answers my prayers—it must be okay that I'm not living right—I'm an exception, a special case,* then think again. There are no special cases when it comes to sin. Sin is always destructive. Because Samson did not conquer his lust when he was young, it conquered him when he was old. The same thing can happen to you and me.

The deception that sin is okay can kill you in the end, even if you enjoy seasons of favor. If you are not where you should be with God, His favor is not supposed to tempt you into deceiving yourself and thinking anything you do is okay with Him. His favor is supposed to bring you to repentance, to where you will say, "God does still love me; God does still want to bless me and use me. I need to repent; I need to get right with God."

The Fallacy of a Trial-Free Future

No one would dispute that the apostle Paul experienced the full force of God's favor. The Lord appeared to Paul on the road to Damascus, called him into the Kingdom, empowered him as the apostle to the Gentiles and inspired him to write most of the New Testament epistles. Did it follow, then, that the more Paul grew in favor, the fewer difficulties he faced? Not at all. Read what Paul recorded about himself in 2 Corinthians 11:23–27 (NLT):

> I have worked harder, been put in jail more often, been whipped times without number, and faced death again and again. Five different times the Jews gave me thirty-nine lashes. Three times I was beaten with rods. Once I was stoned. Three times I was shipwrecked. Once I spent a whole night and a day adrift at sea. I have traveled many weary miles. I have faced danger from flooded rivers and from robbers. I have faced danger from my own people, the Jews, as well as from the Gentiles. I have faced danger in the cities, in the deserts, and on the stormy seas. And I have faced danger from men who claim to be Christians but are not. I have lived with weariness and pain and sleepless nights. Often I have been hungry and thirsty and have gone without food. Often I have shivered with cold, without enough clothing to keep me warm.

You may be thinking, *That doesn't sound like a life of favor to me!* It is a fallacy to think that enjoying favor means you are looking forward to a trial-free future. That is a dangerous train of thought because when adversity comes, you think God has abandoned you. But as I said earlier, adversity is a part of any life—favored or not.

Favor does not prevent adversity. Favor opens a door from adversity into victory. Remember the time Paul was shipwrecked and had to swim for shore? (See Acts

27–28.) He landed on the island of Malta, where the inhabitants kindled a fire and welcomed Paul and the others from the ship. Paul had been a prisoner on board, and when the ship was going down the soldiers almost killed the prisoners to prevent their escape. A centurion intervened, so Paul faced the violent waves instead, struggling to make it to land. Thinking he was momentarily safe once he made it ashore, Paul went off to gather a bundle of sticks. As he added his sticks to the blaze and warmed himself, a viper was driven out of the sticks to escape the heat and fastened itself onto his hand.

Was Paul favored of God? Certainly. God had just protected him from death by shipwreck and death by sword. Was Paul trial-free? Not at all. He now had a poisonous snake hanging off the end of his arm.

Paul had a choice to make in that moment of adversity. He could have thought, *That's it—I've had enough! I thought God was with me, but clearly He has forsaken me. I give up; I'm a dead man anyway.* And likely he would have keeled over and died. That is what the natives were waiting for: "They were expecting that he would swell up or suddenly fall down dead" (Acts 28:6).

Instead Paul shook the viper into the fire and suffered no ill effects. Why? He chose to believe God was *for him.* He knew God had provided a table for him in the presence of his enemies (see Psalm 23:5) and that the presence of an enemy (whether man or viper) did not indicate the absence of God and His provision. Paul kept right on expecting favor, and he got it—too much favor, in fact, from Malta's inhabitants. When they saw no harm befell him from the snakebite, they decided he was a god! Then he had to convince them he did not deserve *that* kind of favor. He healed the island's sick, preached and led the inhabitants to the Savior. He made the most of every opportunity to spread the Gospel, and favor opened doors for Paul from adversity into victory.

Think about Job and the troubles he suffered, or David and his difficulties while Saul was still king. Think about Abraham and Noah and the challenges they faced. Or Joseph, who faced trial after trial. Of all the men and women of God mentioned in Scripture, you would be hard-pressed to find anyone who did not encounter major trials and difficulties. The key to their success was their realization that God could turn any situation around. Job was a prime example. When his wife told him to curse God and die, he instead thanked God, saying, "You have granted me life and favor, and Your care has preserved my spirit" (Job 10:12). In Job's lowest moments, his confession for favor did not falter.

Favor Turns Trouble Around

If you think favor will bring your troubles to an end, you are dreaming, but it *is* true that God can turn the most nightmarish situation around for your benefit. Start to view your troubles as opportunities for God to show you favor in new ways. He can bring good out of any bad and bring you through it into victory. Even when disaster seems to loom ahead, God has a good plan in mind for you.

Many of us can quote Romans 8:28: "And we know that all things work together for good to those who love God, to those who are the called according to His purpose." It is one thing to quote such truths but quite another to believe them. I had to learn early on as a pastor that God could turn great troubles into great victories, but the lesson did not come without difficulties.

Several years ago, back when we had about fifteen hundred people in our congregation, we simply had no room to grow. Our building was small, and on weekends we held a Saturday night service, four Sunday morning services and two Sunday night services. There was not time or room to accommodate anyone new. Right next to our eight acres of land, though, were another ten acres we heard were likely to be put up for sale someday. *This is it!* I thought. *God is going to provide for our growth!*

We found out what those ten acres were worth, and we offered it to the school district that owned the land. "No, we're not interested" was the firm reply. We added a couple hundred thousand dollars and made them another offer. "Not interested," we heard again.

We need that land! I kept thinking. *We're landlocked, and we have to get that extra room to build!*

We made another offer. "Just tell us what you want for the property, and we'll pay it," we wrote. "Name your price!"

"No, we're just not interested in selling right now."

I was devastated. I did not understand. We were completely stuck, and I had no idea what else to do. I also had no idea God was about to turn my disappointment around. His plans were far bigger than mine. About that time, we heard of a businessman who had *138 acres* he wanted to sell. The land was perfectly situated, and we were able to purchase it within a short period of time. Since then, we have gone through several expansions onsite. We have exits on three major roads, acres of parking, magnificent grounds and everything else we could ask for, and *still* we have all the room we need to grow.

Today I shudder when I think of how stuck we could have been, had we gotten that ten acres I had my heart set on. All I can say is, "Thank You, God, that we *didn't* get that land I was so disappointed about. I had no idea what a future You had in mind for us!" Had we stayed where we were and added a few more acres, we could never have ministered to the thousands who now attend our services every weekend.

You might be in one of the darkest or most disappointing times of your life, but do not think that because you have trouble, God has withdrawn His favor or forsaken you. Favor does not eliminate trouble, but it does open the door into victory. Do as Job and David did—confess God's favor more than ever. Realize that God is preparing to pour it out on you more forcefully than you can imagine. His plans for you are far bigger than your own.

Step into Your Promised Land

Now that you are aware of the dangers that accompany favor, do your best to avoid them. Pull out any roots of bitterness before they take hold so that you do not fall from favor. Guard against the "Look at Me!" syndrome and do not allow yourself to take credit for the things God's favor has done in your life. Avoid envying others who enjoy great favor—instead, rejoice with them. Sow favor toward others and you will reap it. Never use favor as an excuse to harbor sin. If your lifestyle does not line up with God's Word, realize His favor is meant to bring you to repentance and draw you back to Him.

Finally, do not let trials and disappointments disillusion you. Shake them off as Paul shook off the viper into the fire, and go on about the business of living for God. Trust that He will favor you with all the blessings His Word promises, and that He has a plan for you far beyond what you can imagine. God's mercies and favor are new every morning. In the face of dangers and difficulties, it may take some effort on your part to start every day expecting, believing for and confessing favor, but that is the path into your Promised Land.

10

Satisfying Your Favor Hunger

It does not matter whether you are a prince or prisoner, young or old, in a factory or in school, living in Africa or England, New York City or Grand Rapids—the favor of God will make you stand out and rise to the top. Whoever and wherever you are, through His favor "the LORD will make you the head and not the tail; you shall be above only, and not be beneath" (Deuteronomy 28:13).

We all share a hunger for that kind of favor from God. An emptiness inside us is filled up and satisfied when we become His children and begin to partake of His many blessings. None of us needs to go hungry when we take God at His Word and realize that the free favors of God profusely abound.

God's people perish for lack of knowledge, according to Hosea 4:6, but the reverse is also true: God's people flourish as they come to know and apply His Word. This is especially true in the area of favor—the more you know, the more you grow. That is why we have spent this time learning how to grow in favor as Jesus did. Favor is far too important for us to go without. It can make all the difference between success and failure.

We have defined favor as "the friendly disposition from which kindly acts proceed; to assist; to provide with special advantages; to receive preferential treatment," and we have discovered the length, breadth and depth of God's favorable disposition toward us. He longs to help us, to provide us with every advantage and to bless us. We are always surrounded by favor, but to realize its full effects we need to hit the switch and turn it on.

We identified the specific steps we can take to "hit the favor switch" and unleash its force in our lives. We know now that when we *expect* that God wants to bless His children, *believe* that His favor is *for us* and *confess* favor with our mouths, He creates the fruit of our lips. Our confession is so vital—a good report that aligns itself with God's Word brings favor our way, while a bad report full of doubt and unbelief can quickly cut off favor's flow. Though favor is not a formula, putting God's Word in our hearts and then speaking it out of our mouths is an unbeatable way to increase our experience of favor.

The Good Taste of Favor

I am continually amazed at the blessings, both big and small, that God releases as I confess His Word and His favor over my life. One day I was eating lunch at a local restaurant with another man from our church. Balanced though I try to be, I admit I have this fetish for ketchup, particularly Heinz ketchup—the kind that comes out extra s-l-o-w. I believe every piece of meat should be baptized—and I do not mean sprinkled—I mean immersed! I thoroughly enjoyed my lunch and my bottle of Heinz ketchup, and then I asked for the bill.

"You won't need to take care of it," said the waitress. She pointed at a man a few tables away. "That man paid for both your lunches."

"I don't recognize him," I told my friend. "Do you know him?"

My friend glanced over and shook his head. "I've never seen him before."

The man who paid for our lunch saw us looking in his direction, so he got up and came over. He held out his business card and said, "I'm the Heinz Ketchup salesman. I have *never* seen anyone enjoy ketchup as much as you do! I just had to buy your lunch."

That is but a small taste of the blessings that favor with God and men has brought into my life. (Although to me, meeting the Heinz ketchup salesman was a big event—who could have a more important job?) But a free lunch was not the only blessing involved in that encounter. We talked a while and invited the Heinz representative to church. He came and got right with God! Watching someone else accept the free gift of salvation and become a child of God is amazing; that is one of the biggest blessings that come my way. God's favor works in marvelous ways.

In these pages we traveled with some of the great men and women of Scripture to observe favor at work in their lives. We followed Naomi's story as she strayed from the course of favor and left the "House of Bread"; then we saw her come back to the place where God's favor could flow to her once again. Ruth stayed the course of favor all along the way and taught us how to move into increased favor. She started at the beginning, as we all do, by accepting the Lord and experiencing salvation—but she did not stop there. As her steps were ordered by the Lord, she began to receive handfuls of favor on purpose.

She learned how to influence those above her and "lead up" with favor, and she saw her requests granted. She also realized that she was meant to share the favor she enjoyed. All of us are blessed to be a blessing—the more favor we sow, the more favor we reap.

We gleaned from the experiences of Joseph and Nehemiah, Job and Paul. We learned from the Old Testament story of the Israelite spies at the border of the Promised Land and the New Testament story of the woman with the issue of blood. From one end of the Bible to the other, we saw powerful demonstrations of how the force of favor works—or does not work—in people's lives.

We found that some dangers can accompany favor. Bitterness, pride and envy can stop favor's flow. And as Samson demonstrated, people can use favor to excuse sin.

People also can interpret trials and adversity as a lack of favor, when actually such times are but opportunities for God to express His favor toward us in new ways. Through favor, He can turn any disappointing circumstance into victory, if we do not become disillusioned and give up.

We have learned much about positioning ourselves so that God can release the full force of His favor toward us, and there will always be much more to learn. I could write another whole book about unleashing the limitless favor of God, but as you begin to apply the principles we have covered here, I pray you will soon have your own stories to tell.

If you have been redeemed by the Lord and you are enjoying His favor, be sure to say so! Tell others how He has poured favor on you, and share your blessings. That is one of the most effective ways to witness—nothing draws people to the Lord like seeing His goodness evidenced in your life. Through you, they can experience some of that favor for themselves. And once they "taste and see that the LORD is good" (Psalm 34:8), they will want to become His children, too.

Taste Favor for Yourself

If you feel that the kind of favor we have talked about in these pages is missing from your life, perhaps you did not realize until now how badly you hungered for the favor of God. If you have not yet experienced the favor that begins with salvation, you can do so today. "Choose for yourselves this day whom you will serve," Joshua 24:15 urges us. If you are among those who have never made Jesus the Lord of their lives, see the appendix that follows this chapter. It will walk you through how to receive salvation so that you can begin to enjoy the favor of God.

Or perhaps you are among the many people I meet who *hope* they are saved and on their way to heaven, but just are not sure. You may believe that you cannot know if you "made it" until you die and stand face-to-face with God. But you do not need to wonder if you are God's child or hope He will adopt you—the Bible says you can *know* it for certain. Do not rest until you know you are in the family of God! I talk more about that in the appendix, too.

Or you may be in a third category—people who became believers but somehow fell away. Maybe you were disillusioned during hard times and gave up on God. He has not given up on you. Even if you have let sin take root in your life and have backed away from Him, He will help you return to the "House of Bread." There His favor can flow to you again. It is never too late to grow! Again, see the appendix for more information.

Whatever category of people you fit into—whether you are a brand-new believer, someone who needs to settle the matter of salvation for sure or someone who needs to return to the Lord—do not wait another minute to get right with the Lord and begin experiencing His favor.

Grow in Divine Favor

I hope these pages have helped you realize the almost unfathomable extent of God's favor toward you. And I hope they have shown you that your longing for favor can be satisfied. You literally can go from a place in your life where you are walking in zero favor to a place where you are walking in 100 percent of the favor God has for you.

Begin to apply these principles we have talked about that surround favor. Once you are on your way, you cannot help but grow in your experience of it. You are already a highly favored child of God who can expect even more favor in your future. Pray for it, thank God for it and speak it out as you call to mind the promises God has given you in His Word and the dreams He has put in your heart.

Grow now in the favor of God and men, as Jesus did. Go boldly ahead to live for Him and rejoice—because ahead of you, behind you and on every side of you is divine favor!

Appendix

Experience Salvation and the Favor of God

When Jesus came, He announced that *now* is the time for the free favors of God to abound profusely (see Luke 4:18–19). If you have not yet experienced that powerful flood of God's favor, then today is your day to begin. God wants to release more favor into your life than you can possibly contain, but it starts right here with experiencing salvation.

In this final section of the book we will walk through exactly how to step into this place where favor begins, becoming a child of God. Before we do that, though, I would like those readers who are not becoming first-time believers to consider something. If you are about to stop reading these pages because you do not think they apply to you, please ask yourself if you are in one of the following categories.

Are you one of the many people I have met who desperately hopes he or she is a child of God, but is not certain of it? When I asked one woman if she was a Christian, she told me, "I am trying to be Christian—I hope I am. I think I am a good person. When I die, I will find out if I made it into heaven, but for now I am doing the best I can."

You do not have to wonder if you are God's child or try to be good enough for Him to accept you. Neither do you make it to heaven based on your own performance, so there is no need to wait until you die to find out what awaits you. In fact, that course of action is dangerous. You cannot live a good enough life, pray enough, fast enough or do enough for others to pay for a ticket to heaven—through His death, burial and resurrection Jesus already accomplished everything needed for you to be saved. Because God gave us eternal life through His Son, you can "know that you have eternal life" (1 John 5:13). If you do not yet know for certain that you are saved, read on and make sure of it.

Are you someone who made a commitment to God and accepted Jesus as Lord and Savior but has since drifted away? Perhaps bitterness, sin or disillusionment set in, and you know you are not where you should be with God anymore. Even if that has been your condition for a very long time, you can come back to Him. Today His favor will flow again toward you. No matter what you have done, you just need to repent and reconnect. Hosea 6:1 urges, "Come, and let us return to the LORD." When you return to the Lord, He will welcome you back with open arms.

In whatever category you find yourself—whether you are a first-time believer, someone who is unsure of where he stands with God or someone who needs to repent and come back to Him—look at what God says about taking you as His child:

In the time of favor (of an assured welcome) I have listened to and heeded your call, and I have helped you on the day of deliverance (the day of salvation). Behold, now is truly the time for a gracious welcome and acceptance [of you from God]; behold, now is the day of salvation!

2 Corinthians 6:2, AMPLIFIED

You are promised an assured welcome in this time of favor. Now is the day of your salvation. God will hear your call.

How do you call on Him? As I said earlier, everything in the Kingdom of God comes the same way. Salvation comes the same way as favor. You expect it, believe it is *for you* and confess it.

First, *expect* in your heart that God wants to save the people He created. His Word assures us that He is "not willing that any should perish but that all should come to repentance" (2 Peter 3:9). Every person on the planet is included in that *all* whom He wishes to come to repentance.

Next, *believe* that His salvation is for you. The Bible promises, "For whosoever shall call upon the name of the Lord shall be saved" (Romans 10:13, KJV). "Whosoever" includes *you*. We are about to pray a prayer of salvation that will work for you, and it works every time!

Finally, *confess* salvation. It needs to be spoken out of your mouth. Romans 10:9 tells us, "If you confess with your mouth the Lord Jesus and believe in your heart that God has raised Him from the dead, you will be saved." Experience salvation and the favor of God right now by confessing with your mouth the following prayer from your heart:

O God, I come to You in Jesus' name.
I believe that Jesus died on the cross,
that He shed His precious blood

and that He paid for my sins.
I receive Your forgiveness for all my sins.

I believe that Jesus rose again,
so right now I receive Him as Lord of my life.
I am not going to live to please myself any longer.
I am going to live for Jesus every day.

Devil, you just lost me.
Jesus, I am Yours.

Heavenly Father, I thank You
that You have heard my prayer.
Thank You that according to Your Word
my sins are forgiven,
my past is gone,
I am Your child,
and I am on my way to heaven!

In Jesus' name,
Amen.

You are now a highly favored child of God. You just made the most important decision of your life, and you will never be the same. You have put yourself in the path of God's favor, and you will begin to see it unleashed in your life in new ways. For a start, you can go to sleep tonight knowing for certain that your sins are forgiven, you are a child of God and you are on your way to heaven.

I do not know of anything more important and exciting than experiencing salvation, yet it is just the beginning of your journey into all the favor God has for you. If you have further questions or need personal assistance to help you on your way, our contact information is listed on my biography page at the back of this book.

Welcome to the family of God!

Pastor Duane Vander Klok, Ph.D., and his wife, Jean, met while attending Christ for the Nations Institute. They served on the mission field for seven years in Mexico with an emphasis on church planting and teaching in Bible schools. In 1984 they accepted the pastorate of Resurrection Life Church (RLC) in Grandville, Michigan.

Resurrection Life has a weekly attendance of approximately eight thousand people with five services each weekend and one midweek service. It also is involved with church planting. Along with overseeing various new churches, Pastor Duane hosts a daily television program called *Walking by Faith* and travels in the United States, Latin America and abroad encouraging the Body of Christ with practical teaching from the Word of God. He is also the author of *Get the Junk Out of Your Trunk* (Chosen, 2005).

Duane and Jean have three sons, Joshua, Samuel and Daniel, and a daughter, Stephanie. Joshua serves as an associate pastor at RLC Grandville. He and his wife, Nancy, have a son Gabe and twins Jazmin and Noah. Samuel and Daniel both serve as assistant pastors in the Youth Department at RLC Grandville. Samuel's wife is Rebecca. Stephanie is currently studying at Hillsong College in Sydney, Australia.

Everyone new in the faith is invited to contact Resurrection Life Church for a complimentary copy of Duane's book *Your New Life*. Call the Prayer Line at 1-800-988-5120 or visit www.walkingbyfaith.org to request a copy. The Prayer Line is also available for sharing prayer needs.